A STUDY OF MANAGEMENT LEADERSHIP QUALITIES WITHIN A NONPROFIT HUMAN SERVICE ORGANIZATION

Doctoral Dissertation Research
Submitted to the Graduate Faculty of
Argosy University, Phoenix Campus
College of Business and Management for
Organizational Leadership

In Partial Fulfillment
of the Requirements for the Degree of
Doctor of Education
Organizational Leadership

DR. SHARON REED

ISBN 978-1-63844-360-5 (paperback)
ISBN 978-1-63844-361-2 (digital)

Copyright © 2021 by Dr. Sharon Reed

All rights reserved. No part of this publication may be reproduced, distributed, or transmitted in any form or by any means, including photocopying, recording, or other electronic or mechanical methods without the prior written permission of the publisher. For permission requests, solicit the publisher via the address below.

Christian Faith Publishing, Inc.
832 Park Avenue
Meadville, PA 16335
www.christianfaithpublishing.com

Printed in the United States of America

A Study of Management Leadership Qualities Within
a Nonprofit Human Service Organization

To the late Mother Betty Campbell, my immediate family and church family, and coworkers, thank you for being there and supporting me through this endeavor and giving me encouragement, guidance, and support. Special thanks to a special person whom I regard as my backbone throughout this process—my Lord and Savior Jesus Christ. When I thought I could not make it, I would go down and pray. I could hear through words you can do all things through Christ Jesus who strengthens you. You can make it. These words helped me throughout my journey.

Thank you, Lord, for allowing me to take this leap of faith and putting all my trust in you to complete this journey.

Abstract

More than a few studies have been completed on leadership; nonetheless, there is a shortage of literature concerning the leadership skills of managers within the human services field. Therefore, this dissertation analyzed the relationships of leadership behaviors (i.e., personal support, objective emphasis, and work easing) to the didactic and professional backgrounds of managers within the human services area. The quantitative research was conducted in a human service organization in Massachusetts utilizing the Leadership—Michigan Organizational Assessment. The outcomes of the study show there was a significant relationship made by managers with a didactic or professional context in human service and the leadership skills of personal support.

Acknowledgments

Many individuals have been a factor in this dissertation in many ways, but I would like to thank and recognize my Lord and Savior, Jesus Christ, for being the head of my life and steering me through this journey and process. My dissertations chair, Dr. Robert Goldwasser, has made available guidance and proffered notions and proposals, which eventually led to the triumphant completion of this dissertation. He offered additional advice to make certain the process would be successful. He helped with selecting committee members with strong points in different areas, which complimented each other and this dissertation superbly. Dissertation committee member Dr. Samara Kramer offered guidance over and above what was anticipated and was willing to give more advice to help find organizations to study.

I would like to acknowledge and thank Dr. Chris White, who allowed me to study his organization Road to Responsibility. He was eager and hospitable to the study of the organization and helped with my dissertation research. He remembered the process and was willing to help me in hopes that it would make my journey on the dissertation path a little easier.

Contents

List of Tables 15
List of Figures 17

Chapter 1: Introduction 19
Introduction to the Study 19
Background of Study 20
    Department of Human Service 21
Statement of the Problem 24
Purpose of the Study 24
Rationale 24
Conceptual Framework 25
Research Questions and Hypotheses 26
Nature of the Study 26
Significance of the Study 27
Assumptions 28
Limitations 29
Definition of Terms 29
Organization of Remaining Chapters 30

Chapter 2: Literature Review 31
Introduction 31
Leadership 32
    Authoritarian 32
    Compromise management 33
    Transformational leadership 34
    Situational leadership 35
    Leader-member exchange 36

Robert House Leadership Theorist 39
Managers and Leaders in a Nonprofit Organization 41
    The role of the manager in a nonprofit organization 43
Organizational Culture 46
Perceptions of Leadership and Management 47
Conclusion 50

Chapter 3: Methodology 51
Introduction 51
Design of the Study 51
Research Questions 52
    Data Collection Instrument: The Nonprofit
    Organizational Leadership Survey 53
Research Instrument 53
Population 55
Sample 56
Dependent Variables 56
Independent Variable 56
Test Factors 57
Reliability and Validity 57
Data Collection Procedure and Coding 59
Data Analysis Plan 60
Research Ethics and Protection of Subjects 60
    Consent form 61
    Limitations 61
    Delimitations 62
Summary 62

Chapter 4: Results 64
Research Questions 65
Data Screening, Reliability, Summated Scales, and
Statistical Tests 65
    Data screening 65
    Reliability 66
    Summated scale scores 66
    Chi-square test of independence 67

Correlations 68
MANCOVA test 68
Demographic Characteristics...70
Descriptive Statistics for Summated Scales and
Managerial Effectiveness..75
Correlations 77
Results for Research Questions 1–3.....................................79
Answer to research questions 83
Ideal Nonprofit Leadership..83
Ideal leadership style for a nonprofit manager.......................84
Best leadership style for a nonprofit organization..................86
Summary...88

Chapter 5: Results, Recommendations, and Limitations 90
Purpose of the Study 90
Summary of Study...92
Discussion, Results, and Conclusions 94
Research question 1...97
Research question 2...97
Research question 3...97
Limitations..98
Implications 100
Recommendations for Future Research 101
Conclusion..103

References 107

List of Tables

Table 1. Manager's Professional Background by Human
Services Education Cross-tabulation 75

Table 2. Descriptive Statistics for Summated Scales and
Managerial Effectiveness 77

Table 3. Pearson Correlation Matrix of Leadership Styles
and Demographic Variables 79

Table 4. Percentages and Corresponding Numbers
of Participants by Ideal Nonprofit Manager
Leadership Styles..86

List of Figures

Figure 1. Numbers of participants by human services degrees.......71
Figure 2. Numbers of participants by ethnicity. 72
Figure 3. Numbers of participants by marital status......................72
Figure 4. Cross-tabulation between human services degree held (yes or no) and the manager's professional background in human services (yes or no). 74
Figure 5. Mean aims emphasis SS across managers with and without a human services degree............................81
Figure 6. Mean personal support SS across managers with and without a human services degree............................82
Figure 7. Mean work easing SS across managers with and without a human services degree. 84
Figure 8. Percentages of participants in three ideal manager leadership styles...85
Figure 9. Percentages of participants in four ideal leadership types for nonprofit organizations. 87

Chapter 1: Introduction

Introduction to the Study

Newman, Guy, and Mastracci (2009) showed that human service employees go through emotive labor. They decided the most momentous challenge before individuals working within the human service field is that workers who happen not to be wasteful in their work have less humane and considerate traits. Leadership in the business industry is a subject that has been extensively analyzed from many points of view. Then again, the nature of leadership in human service organizations is a subject with greater dynamics. Most human service organizations are nonprofit because the founders of the organizations are concerned with serving people who have restricted means.

The makeup of many nonprofit human service organizations is as follows: group residences and halfway residences; correctional, cerebral disability, and public mental health centers; family, children, and youth service bureaus; and programs concerning intoxication, substance misuse, domestic aggression, and the elderly. The area of human services is generally defined, distinctively approaching the objective of encountering human wants through an interdisciplinary knowledge base, concentrating on prevention in addition to remediation of difficulties, and preserving a dedication to enhancing the general quality of life of service populations. The human services organization is one that further enhanced service delivery techniques by addressing not just the quality of direct services but also by looking to enhance user-friendliness, answerability, and coordination among workers and bureaus in service delivery.

Various human service organizations follow the pyramid makeup, which unifies concluding authority in one manager. Characteristically, the pyramid structure identifies two well-defined business processes, administration and supervisory. At one end, the manager supervises administrative functions with the aid of exceptional assistants (Department of Human Services, Dane County 2008). There are usually boards of directors. Below the board of directors is the chief executive officer, who oversees the middle and lower-level managers who supervise the workers. The managers and the supervisors are the main points of communication for the family members and custodians of the persons obtaining services. They supervise a caseload and make certain that every individual is getting suitable, high-quality services. They also oversee the direct-care providers. As a result of the double role managers carry, they are in the position that this study addresses because the two roles require different kinds of administrative, organizational, and leadership skills.

Background of Study

This study sought to establish the leadership skills managers in nonprofit human service organizations obtain. Persons who decide to work in the field of human services as part of their vocation are characteristically caring and unselfish individuals because the intention of their work is to enhance the lives of others in addition to the salaries, which are significantly lower than those of careers with comparable levels of responsibility and didactic requirements in for-profit organizations (Dias and Maynard-Moody 2007). Therefore, the managers of human service organizations possess different challenges than managers of other organizations because the culture of the companies is very reliant upon interpersonal relationships made by workers and clients. The human service business is multifaceted and entails decisions made by government, social, and organizational leaders (Glisson 1978). Within the human service, manufactured goods are not sold; but a service is provided for persons with disabilities, families who require extra support, individuals with psychological illnesses, and persons with drug and alcohol dependence.

A STUDY OF MANAGEMENT LEADERSHIP QUALITIES WITHIN A NONPROFIT HUMAN SERVICE ORGANIZATION

The ethos of the organizations that provide these services are frequently different from organizations that manufacture a product to be sold since these organizations spend a considerable amount of time with the clients of these services (Shapiro and Hassinger 2007). This kind of employment is not suited for every individual because of the culture that exists in the field (DelCampo 2006). An organization builds on its organizational culture over time. As the organization develops, the culture is less likely to be influenced by the addition or subtraction of one worker. Therefore, it is significant for new workers to fit into the existing culture since it is less probable that the culture will adjust to them (Weinberg 2005). Within the human service field, the culture may be fashioned by the mission of the company. The goal of the administrators and managers is to carry out the mission of the organization, which is frequently focused on helping a particular population in the most well-organized and effective way possible.

Department of Human Service

Throughout numerous organizations, the human services sector makes available healthiness, education, and welfare from cradle to grave. Human services are comprehensive interdisciplinary fields with an obligation to enhance the general excellence of life in varied populations through meeting basic human wants and alleviating social difficulties. Frequently referred to as social amenities, human services involve the occupations that provide services to people, especially on occasions of vulnerability or crisis. Human services workers abet others in finding a way through frustrating states of affairs to overcome obstructions, find their self-adequacy again, and move forward in their lives. A human service usually includes service work in government extensions, nonprofit organizations, social service agencies, private practices, hospitals, and mental health centers. Human service businesses make available housing, vocational, conveyance, and psychological-healthiness support to persons with developmental disabilities, physical disabilities, psychological well-being, in addition to disadvantaged persons and families (Greene and Burke

2007). The ethos of organizations within the human service field is extremely unlike any other organization. Therefore, it is significant to be aware of the derivation of these policies that organizations within the human service field are required to pursue. The policies, because of their inflexibility, as well as the monetary support from the Department of Human Services, serve a function in creating the ethos in the many organizations they influence.

The upbeat purpose of the Department of Human Services is that it is a way to systematize public services subsidized by local governments. The organization accepts money allocated by means of the national or county fiscal plan. Not-for-profit organizations involve organizations that might accept considerable community funding, but that remain privately managed and under the guidance of an executive board with everyday management by a director. Any profits accruing to these organizations either go back into the agency's budget or are returned to the funding supply. It then handles the funds to make the most of the number of persons who are able to benefit from the funds allocated. The company also gives a suite of controls to make certain that individuals are in receipt of the services they require in a suitable way. This means the coffers are utilized to employ the most answerable persons to give the most effective services to those within the population ("Department of Human Services, Dane County" 2008). They are very reliant on outside contributors to put money into their organization that brings them into increasingly complex relationships with their task surroundings (Weisbrod 1997).

Currently, there are a significant number of dysfunctional aspects to this system of government (Havighurst et al. 2001), such as the time clients wait before receiving services. Not only does the application take time to be approved, but then the person must wait until the information is verified. This may leave the individual with no assistance for quite some time. Also, this takes time because everything has to go through a long chain of command, which indirectly causes people to suffer. Funding is another dysfunctional aspect of the program. There are many organizations within the Department of Human Services that require funding. When human service budgets shrink, a conservative political climate is created or reinforced, leading to a retrenchment in spending on human services by governmental and private sources. The department has a limit on the funds that can be dispersed, which does not allow some organizations to receive funding. These are issues directors and managers must address in their role in managing the budget.

The employees who work in the human services organizations have the privilege of being able to help others through their jobs (Weber 2007). Whenever a program is developed or maintained, that program helps numerous people. One aspect of the department is to allocate funding to people with developmental disabilities so they can purchase services from private companies. This funding allows these people to reside in group homes with assistance from support workers. The amount of assistance each individual needs is determined on a case-by-case basis. This determination is also the role of the director.

Directors working in the department or private companies are also pressured because the funding available for programs is very limited (Cosmides and Tooby 2004). They must allocate money based on priority, which can be difficult when many of the programs are equally important. Also, employees may want programs to progress quickly because they are able to help more people this way; but due to the structure and requirements the government has imposed upon them, efficiency is not always possible. The requirements people must go through are necessary to prevent fraud by people who do not require services.

The customers of these types of organizations are people in the community who rely on support from the government because they would not be able to function successfully in the community without assistance ("Department of Human Services, Dane County" 2008). These groups include people with disabilities, people with drug and alcohol problems, people who need social assistance, and a variety of other groups. The lives of these people are affected on a daily basis due to the decisions that are made and guidelines the department puts in place. If people did not receive services, they would either be on their own or find other nonstructured ways to receive support such as homelessness and crime.

Statement of the Problem

In an extensive search of the literature, there was a deficiency of literature with reference to the leadership qualities of individuals in supervisory positions within nonprofit human service organizations. Weber (2007) discovered more research should be conducted in this area. There is a need for more knowledge about leadership qualities and their implications in the human service field (Bargal and Schmid 1989, Glisson 1989). The persons in managerial positions within these agencies usually possess an educational background in the field of human services with minimal education in management and leadership (Weber 2007). Therefore, the problem in this study was the difficulty managers within the human service field have when they manage both consumer care and workers. The survey utilized in this study identified three factors directors should process to be effective managers and directors.

Purpose of the Study

The intention of this study was to decide if any essential leadership qualities are deficient in managers of nonprofit human service organizations. The purpose of identifying these factors was to make managers and their supervisors conscious of this necessity. Actions may be taken to correct these areas and make the managers well-informed professionals. This was a quantitative study conducted by surveying workers of nonprofit human service organizations to determine the perceptions of the leadership qualities of their managers.

Rationale

The outcomes of this study will help existing organizations in giving training to existing managers or direct them in employing and promoting managers with human service backgrounds to upper managing positions. Therefore, both the persons receiving services from the organization, as well as the subordinates of the managers, will be supervised well. This may help in decreasing the renewal rate of workers in organizations within the human service field.

Conceptual Framework

For many years, authors have been fascinated with the notion of stipulating foreseeable relations made by what an organization's leaders do and in what way the organization manages (Institute for Social Research 1975). Four dimensions emerged from these investigations that include the basic structure of what one might call leadership: there is a call for more education and ability concerning leadership, as well as its implications within the human services field (Bargal and Schmid 1989, Glisson 1989). Glisson declared that whereas aspects of management are essential for the performance of institutions, leadership cultivates an organizational climate and ethos within which employees may perform. Glisson thinks it is this effect that makes leadership significant within nonprofit human service organizations, as employees are thought of as their primary asset. He asserted leadership might add to workplace self-worth, decrease employee burnout, gain the most from individual promise, and therefore, meet the objectives of the institution better. Whereas these leading experts wrote of this matter more than a decade ago, little has been found in the current literature from the human service point of view.

- *Support*: behavior that improves someone else's emotion of individual value and significance.
- *Interaction easing*: behavior that gives confidence to members of the group to build on close, mutually fulfilling relationships.
- *Objective emphasis*: behavior that stimulates a passion for meeting the group's objective or accomplishing excellent performance.
- *Work easing*: behavior that helps accomplish goal achievement by such activities as scheduling, organizing, plan-

ning, as well as making available resources (for instance, tools, substance, and technological ability).

Research Questions and Hypotheses

The research question this study concentrated on was, which three leadership activities (i.e., personal support, objective emphasis, and work easing) do human service managers process, and what essential qualities are deficient? Therefore, the following hypothesis has been devised based on the research inquiry.

$H1_A$: compared to those with other degrees, human service managers with human service degrees or preceding background place greater emphasis on goals.

$H1_0$: compared to those with no degrees, human service managers with degrees or preceding background process the same emphasis on goals.

$H2_A$: compared to those with human service degrees, human service managers with no degrees and only human services experience place greater emphasis on personal support.

$H2_0$: compared to those with human service degrees, human service managers with no degrees and only human services experience place the same emphasis on personal support.

$H3_A$: compared to those with no human service degrees, human service managers with degrees or previous background place more emphasis on work easing.

$H3_0$: compared to those with no human service degrees, human service managers with human service degrees or preceding background place the same emphasis on work easing.

Nature of the Study

The intention of this quantitative, nonexperimental, explanatory, correctional study was to determine answers to the inquiries and construct a database utilizing the best method (Creswell 2003). When determining a research method, the inquiry asked in the study should explicate the kind of research method to be utilized.

The quantitative research method has more than a few strong points, counting the capacity to examine large quantities of data, ascertain independent and reliant variables, manufacture statistic evaluations that give details to the significance of the data, as well as the capacity to demonstrate if the results of a study are valid and authoritative (Creswell 2003). The quantitative method entails gathering data that may be assessed with statistics. Therefore, the data should be numbers or have the capacity to be allocated significant numbers that may help in dispensing the data. This allowed for factor investigation, cluster investigation, multivariate, as well as explanatory statistics utilizing the SPSS encode.

Surveys are useful for answering close-ended inquiries (Fowler 2002). This may give information that can be categorized on a Likert scale that is helpful for attaining quantitative data.

Significance of the Study

It is essential for nonprofit human service organizations to ascertain which leadership qualities their managers do not have (Weber 2007). This may help in either training present managers to obtain missing skills; or when upcoming managers are promoted or employed, the company may have as a feature of leadership skills as nonexchangeable building blocks essential in the potential applicants.

If human service companies hire managers with leadership skills and ability of the human service business, the outcome is beneficial to the staff, those served by the company, and the company itself (Weber 2007). A strong manager may help decrease worker turnover, as well as help in training staff to provide high-quality service. It will also provide the staff with a better scale of job fulfillment. When staff members are content with their jobs, they are more likely to do the job well and to remain with the organization. Strong leadership may aid the company. Human service companies are characteristically nonprofit ("Department of Human Services, Dane County" 2008). This denotes there are restricted resources. When clients come to the organization for assistance, they have money allocated to them from their state, which gives financial support to the company. If strong leadership helps construct the reputation of the company, it can appeal to more clients and add to the cash flow of the company. In turn, this may allow the company to offer more services. If they believe their family is being taken care of, it will also aid some clients' family members. If the staff members are working with the clients for an extended period, the families may become familiar with the staff and trust them and the work they do.

This research also is relevant since it might encourage educational organizations to have leadership courses as a management feature, which lead to leadership in the human service field (Weber 2007). Such a course could be a prerequisite for human service learners. The courses could explain how to manage both staff and a workload at the same time, as the position requires outstanding managerial and organizational skills.

Assumptions

Assumptions are based on the blueprint of the study. It is essential to make a note of the assumptions utilized when relating both the study and results since these assumptions should be considered when a conclusion is made:

1. This study presupposed managers directly oversee employees.
2. It also presupposed that the educational background of managers is in a human service area.
3. It presupposed that every response to the survey was from a staff member in the human service field.
4. The population sampled was symbolic of every staff member within a human service company.
5. The data-entry procedure precisely recorded the data from the survey to the data reading format.

Limitations

The limitations of this study are as follows. Similar to the suppositions, the limitations should be well-thought-out when drawing conclusions based upon the investigation of the research.

1. The limitations of the study include that it surveyed a single nonprofit human service organization in Massachusetts. The qualities that management and human resources seek within this company might be unlike those of organizations in other areas.
2. The response rate might have been a potential constraint if a low proportion of surveys had happened to be returned.

Definition of Terms

The following are definitions of terminology that were utilized throughout the study:

- *Consumers.* A consumer is an individual who meets the criteria for services ("Department of Human Services, Dane County" 2008). This may well be due to disability, psychosis, socioeconomic status, drug/alcohol dependence, or a combination of these reasons.
- *Human service managers.* Managers in human service organizations are the staff who fill positions within the human service organizations, which are accountable for the employees of consumers and the supervision of staff that give direct services to the consumers (Glisson 1978).
- *Leadership.* Leadership consists of "managerially helpful activities by one member of an organizational relation in the direction of one more associate or associates of the identical organizational family" (Bowers and Seashore 1966). Leadership is also the capability to inspire others based on traits and skills. The reason for utilizing leadership skills is to inspire associates of a company to work

jointly to accomplish a shared goal. These skills are also innate or learned.
- *Nonprofit.* An organization that typically has little financial support to get to the goal and does not propose to make a profit (Glisson 1978).
- *Organization.* A grouping of individuals who come together to arrive at a shared goal (Daft 2005).

Organization of Remaining Chapters

Chapter 1 offered an introduction and background of the analysis, problem, purpose statement, rationale, research questions, hypotheses, conceptual framework, a definition, assumptions, limitations, as well as the importance of the study. The second chapter provides a literature review of leadership practices and hypotheses. It also assesses the literature available regarding human service management. It provides the underlying principle for the research discussed in this dissertation. The third chapter provides details on the methodology that was utilized in the research. An underlying principle was given for a quantitative study as the best method for this research. It also described the population studied and the legality and soundness of the research procedure and tools being used. The fourth chapter presents the analysis of data that was carried out by utilizing SPSS analysis software. The last section provides the data analysis, advice for upcoming studies, and advice on how the results may be interpreted and put into operation in higher learning. Through the remaining sections of this dissertation, statistical information is utilized to establish whether further preparation of human service managers both in secondary education and company-based training is necessary.

Chapter 2: Literature Review

Introduction

The following literature review concentrates on four particular ranges of study related to the background of this research: leadership overview, nonprofit leadership management, organizational ethos, and employee perceptions of management (University of Michigan 1975). It is vital to evaluate organizational ethos since the background of many human service organizations is distinctive from that of corporate organizations (Dittrich and Carrell 1979). This is pertinent to the study since it denotes that the assumptions found in the data analysis can only be useful to organizations in the human service field. Leadership was reviewed since it is imperative to the achievement of any company. The leadership abilities of managers within the human service industry should indicate the leadership qualities that have been discussed in determining works, as these skills have been useful in an array of distinct types of organizations (Weber 2007). At last, a broad analysis of leadership perceptions was performed since the reason for the research was shaping how the leadership skills of managers affect their employees. The result was that subordinates' understanding was mainly based on the opinions of their management and their managerial skills (Meers 2007). The majority of leadership research has been conducted in regular companies or public-sector organizations in the business world. However, the research on leadership in nonprofit organizations has been scarce even though these organizations play an important part in society and the economy as well. It is argued that leadership in nonprofit organizations is different from that of a commercial organization.

What leadership skills do managers have? The research question of this study was, therefore, how do leadership skills affect person support, goal emphasis, and work facilitation among human service managers, and what essential traits are they needing or lacking?

Leadership

Leadership has been defined in terms of individual traits, behavior, influence over other people, interaction patterns, role relationship, an administrative position, and perception of others regarding the legitimacy of influence (Yukl 1989).

While exploring the labor force, it was apparent there were a lot of different kinds of leadership styles. A number of persons are very authoritarian whereas others lead by example or by cooperating (Bolman and Deal 2003). Every leadership style may be observed in various ways through the different organizational frameworks. One manner might be through the structural makeup and the emblematic frame whereas another style might be totally opposed. Looking through the different frames when assessing different leadership styles may lend a hand to ascertain which style an individual should endeavor to employ or which manner to look for within a leader when looking at filling a new position (Maak 2007). If an individual is in a leadership position, either officially or unofficially, he or she can ask subordinates to assess the leadership style by means of the four different frames to ascertain if the leader perceives the style correctly.

Authoritarian

Leaders who have an authoritarian management style have a great concern for task and less concern for people (Bolman and Deal 2003). Employees who work with managers using the authoritarian managing approach typically have a difficult time working with this type of manager.

After considering the four frames (structural, human resources, political, and symbolic), a person using the authoritarian management style appears very strong in the structural frame because it is associated with confidence and sometimes can be perceived as arrogance by others (Bolman and Deal 2003). An individual using this approach has a clear understanding of who is in the chain of authority, how to complete a task proficiently and successfully, and has excellent organizational skills. This approach has little concern for employees.

Seeing management via the political frame, it is difficult to declare whether people who use an authoritarian approach will seem strong or weak. The political frame focuses on power conflicts and alliances (Bolman and Deal 2003). If someone under the supervision confronts a leader's power, the leader may seem strong via the political structure since the power will not be passed on to the subordinate. If groups are being formed within the organization, an individual with the authoritative management approach should not get employees involved because his or her only concern should be completing the tasks of the organization.

Like the human resources frame, the authoritative management style appears to be weak through the symbolic frame; the symbolic frame looks at customs, rituals, and symbols of an organization (Bolman and Deal 2003). None of these traits appear to be vital to a person exercising the authoritative management approach since all the attention is on completing the tasks.

Compromise management

Leaders who have a compromise management style have a moderate concern for the task and moderate concern for people (Bolman and Deal 2003). This kind of manager attempts to alleviate the importance of completing the task while connecting to the subordinates and keeping them pleased since the team is usually effective and they get along with the manager. The manager obtains respect because he or she listens to the subordinates and incorporates their ideas.

Through the structural frame, the compromise management approach is relatively strong. There is an emphasis on completing the task. However, if there is a personal issue with an employee, this type of leader allows for some leniency even if it means the task is not accomplished in the most efficient manner (Bolman and Deal 2003). The human resource frame also demonstrates that the compromise management style is moderately strong (Bolman and Deal 2003). This kind of manager will adapt his or her needs for the employees provided it does not cause the task to be neglected. If the task is put aside by the employees for a period of time, the manager will not become distressed. The political frame shows this approach to be impartial. This type of leader will try to avoid power struggles because he or she will try to keep employees happy (Bolman and Deal 2003). Alternatively, managers will not let subordinates take advantage of them because they may discourage the workers from completing the tasks. It is possible this kind of manager will discover a way to work together with the employees to reduce the power struggle without becoming defensive.

The compromise management style appears to be the weakest through the symbolic frame (Bolman and Deal 2003). A great deal of consideration is given to the workers in keeping them happy so they can complete the task. Therefore, it is difficult to give significant importance to symbols and rituals. The leader might recognize them but will not automatically be extremely concerned with them. A subordinate would almost certainly want to work with a leader who uses the compromise management approach rather than the authoritative management approach since more emphasis will be given to the workers. Of all the management styles, the integrative style appears to be the most useful because it shows a high concern for both subordinates and for finishing the task.

Transformational leadership

Leaders who have a transformational management style are involved with feelings, morals, values, and long-term objectives. Northouse (2001) inferred that transformational leadership entails an outstanding form of impact, which moves supporters to achieve more than what is typically anticipated of them. Frequently, the leadership style includes charismatic and prophetic leadership. With transformational leadership, supporters feel trust, admiration, and allegiance. They are inspired to do their best for higher order objectives rather than pursue their current interests. A potential effect of transformational leadership is the self-actualization of managers and supporters. Transformational leadership takes extreme measures to accomplish more and to inspire supporters to accomplish more (Arnold et al. 2007, Bass 1998, Bass and Riggio 2006). Arnold et al. (2007) abstracted the four types of transformational management as idealized impact, inspiring impact, intellectual stimulation, and personalized thoughtfulness.

Transformational managers are more likely to be established in organizations wherein objectives and structures are indistinct, but affection and trust are high (Conger 1999). Jones (2006) defined transformational managers as persons who instill in their workers a meaning of function more than task focus. Jones alleged that because of this style of leadership, people are changed into better individuals, therefore, producing greater value for their organizations.

Situational leadership

Leaders who have a situational leadership management style are rooted in the communication among the dimensions of relationship activities and task activities, in addition to employees' willingness or maturity in favor of performing a particular task (Hersey and Blanchard 1996). Employees are the essential aspect of management events. Therefore, as employees change, so does the appropriate technique of management. Northouse (2001) reported that situational leadership examines how managers may turn out to be efficient in many different kinds of organizational surroundings relating to a broad diversity of everyday organizational jobs. Further, a knowledge activity includes informing individuals about what to carry out, how to carry it out, where to carry it out, and when to carry it out and subsequently broadly oversee their achievement, though supportive activities include paying attention to individuals, giving support, and backing up for their efforts, making their participation in problem-solving easy, and making decisions (Blanchard, 1991). Northouse (2001) demonstrated that the efficiency of leadership occurs when the manager has a diagnosis of the progress level of employees in a task state and then displays the recommended leadership style that goes with that state of affairs.

Leader-member exchange

Leaders who have a leader-member exchange (LMX) management style concentrate on a dyad, which is the relationship a manager has with every subordinate in the group. Every connection, or relationship, is probably different in quality. Therefore, the same manager might process poor interpersonal relationships with a number of subordinates and open and trusting relationships with others. The relations surrounded by these combinations, or dyads, might exist of a primarily in-group or out-group character. A manager begins either an in-group or an out-group exchange among members of the organization near the beginning of the dyadic affiliation. Affiliates of the in-group are asked to partake in decision making as well as are delegating additional tasks. The manager lets these affiliates have certain leeway within their roles; in fact, the manager and the principal subordinates bargain the latter's tasks in a noncontractual barter association. Basically, an in-group member is raised to the unofficial function of "entrusted lieutenant." In-group affiliates, in a lot of respects, like the advantages of job leeway (control in decision-making, open infrastructure, self-assurance, and gaining favor with the supervisor). The subordinate usually gives in return with higher than normal expenditures of time and effort, the possibility of more responsibility, and dedication to the success of the establishment. On the contrary, members of the out-group are supervised within fine restrictions of their official employment agreement. Authority is gained via the understood agreement by the employee and the organization. The manager will provide support and help though mandated by way of obligation but will not go further than such restrictions. In fact, the manager works a contractual exchange among such employees (Graen and Cashman 1975).

A STUDY OF MANAGEMENT LEADERSHIP QUALITIES WITHIN A NONPROFIT HUMAN SERVICE ORGANIZATION

Kotter (1990) discussed the need for leaders to be motivational and confident. For one individual to do what is asked of another, the person who is asking must have authority of some type. The power either comes from having a position of power or gaining respect from being well-informed, understanding, and self-assured (Bolman and Deal 2003). In a number of cases, leaders have a mixture of these kinds of power. Within the human service field, new subordinates are quite often fearful of making errors, whether it is a medication occurrence or giving the incorrect support or advice to a consumer. In these states of affairs, they often call a manager or someone who has been at the company for a more extended period to make sure they are doing the task correctly or to get a second opinion (Maak 2007).

In most residential settings, workers often work on their own without seeing a manager or other employees for days or, on occasion, weeks at a time. The majority of the communication takes place on the phone, so the managers need to communicate their needs well to ensure workers understand what they need to do and then follow up with the consumers to check if the employee is doing the job correctly ("Department of Human Services, Dane County" 2008).

Wren (1995) also disputed that leadership, for the most part, is learned by many people. This is a questionable dispute that begins to examine the nature-versus-nurture argument. Real leaders are most apt to learn some of their skills all through their lives whether it is from choosing how to initiate a game on a playground or from seeing another manager use methods to encourage others. However, it should also be noticed that some individuals are born with traits that help them in growing into a leader (Bolman and Deal 2003). Individuals who are innately outgoing with outstanding communication skills and who are sympathetic may well be more able to motivate employees than other supervisors who work to expand these skills. It appears the greatest leaders will have a combination of positive personality traits and knowledge of life that have taught them how to successfully inspire and support others to achieve specific actions. This lets the subordinates to be drawn to the leaders for guidance; however, at the same time, the leaders are eager to learn new skills to continually develop their leadership abilities. Leaders are not always managers; however, an organization hopes to be able to determine which workers have the leadership skills that, if promoted, would remain valuable to the organization.

Wren (1995) examined the various types of leadership, how people are investigating what leadership is, and how they distinguish between these types to discover an accurate understanding of leadership. A leader can be thought of as someone who has made remarkable changes, for example, some presidents of the United States. Lincoln brought the country out of slavery. This was an immensely disliked decision; therefore, it took a great deal to persuade the states that slaves should be afforded better lives. There are other leaders who were not chosen and then decided by people emulating them and looking to them as a leader based on the way they have led their lives. For example, a woman at church started creating quilts to give to the homeless shelter. She did not broadcast what she was undertaking; and then once others found out, they were motivated by similar actions. Leaders can try to generate a change before they can bring about a change on a smaller level. This is one of the problems in explaining leadership. A person's achievement can cause effects in others whether intended or not.

The study of leadership is sometimes disputed. It is difficult for someone to describe precisely what leadership is. Some decide not to include the topic in their course load (Wren 1995). Many other people think the workplace should be moving toward using teams and equality. A leader can be viewed negatively as a manager who works contrary to the goal of equality (Bolman and Deal 2003). However, still in a team setting, there is more often a person or group of people who help design project plans and help assign which team members will play a role in completing the project. This person does not need to have the title of leader; however, that person is carrying out the role of a leader.

One perception that all managers share is the skill to inspire, whether by means of actions or words. The ability to inspire can come by way of respect for expertise and dealings. No matter what actions a manager uses, the action inspires others to take corresponding actions.

Robert House Leadership Theorist

Robert House developed a remarkable leadership concept with the ability to adapt to the needs of subordinates. By means of focusing on what inspires each employee, managers can seek out those with needs and wants and give directions that will influence every subordinate to his or her desired individual purpose and, at the same time, help them turn out to be more productive, as well as work more successfully toward the goal of the organization. There are some drawbacks, particularly for a manager with little or no experience. But depending on the conditions, these challenges can also be conquered, or else the theory can be adjusted to fix the situation. House has developed a hypothesis that is entirely about modification.

Robert House developed the path-goal hypothesis. This theory explains what a manager must do to attain high production and morale (Dubrin 2004). The manager accomplishes this by reviewing each member or employee of the team to help guide them so the individual's goals are reached. This theory gives emphasis on adapting one's leadership style to inspire each person to his or her best ability.

Path-goal theory goes on to show the various leadership styles that can be used with various people. The first is the directive approach. This is when the leader places importance on organization, planning, and controlling, particularly when the final goal is uncertain.

Next is the supported approach when a leader is supposed to show interest in the employees and offer emotionally supportive surroundings. The participative approach is when the leader asks the other employees or group for their ideas before making decisions. Last, the accomplishment-oriented style is when the manager places several goals and high expectations on the team.

Strength of theory. This theory has a number of strong points. The most vital one is that House considered people to be different. Therefore, everyone is inspired by various things; and when approached by management, everyone has different comfort levels. There are other excellent theories; however, they do not always work for each person. For example, an employee who needs emotional support most likely would not benefit from the accomplishment-oriented approach or the directive approach of management because these approaches focus more on getting the job completed and the inherent inspiration of doing well at the job instead of satisfying everyone's sense of worth.

Another strong point of this approach is that it suggests names and descriptions of various leadership styles that may be utilized to inspire other employees. It can be easier to agree on how to treat a subordinate after assessing the various styles and then making a formal decision on which style might best fit this person.

Weakness of theory. Although this approach does an excellent job covering how to be a good manager to various types of employees and group members, it can cause a small number of problems between the groups themselves. By dealing with employees in a different way based on their needs, the employees may as well have the same outcome of reaching the personal and professional goal, but they may become envious or offended by each other if they see a leader behaving differently toward them. They might believe the leader gave special treatment to others.

In addition, it could become challenging and emotionally demanding for a manager to attempt to get to know each employee or team member well enough to choose what inspires each of them. With some employees, it is easy to decide the kind of support they need; but with other employees, it may be more difficult to determine what actually inspires each of them.

If the manager needs to talk to a group of people on some occasion, for example, in a staff meeting, it will not be possible to deal with each employee in a different way. This makes applying this theory difficult, however, not impossible. A skilled manager can find ways to integrate all styles of leadership and management ability into a meeting or speech.

Application of theory. This concept appears as though it can be applied to many types of organizations. Mainly in organizations where there is repetitive work, this theory would work very well since there are many different people with various backgrounds and, therefore, various needs and motivators. One person may stay employed at the job to pay the bills and have no particular interest in the work. If the manager is conscious of this, he or she could use the achievement-oriented approach to help make the work more stimulating by establishing small goals. Other people might have low self-assurance, so the manager could help those people by using the supportive approach and give them jobs that they thrive in to help develop their confidence.

New concepts. There are two new ideas learned from this model. The first is the idea of a manager performing in various ways with various people. It may be difficult for certain people to alter their styles so rapidly; however, it may come more easily depending on the type of person with whom they are connecting.

House appears to be one the most ingenious and groundbreaking leadership theorists because he took portions of other theories and turned them into a set of approaches that could be utilized by one leader and make the best use of the productivity of all employees. It should have taken quite some consideration to form such a complex theory since it involves so many parts. Many times, challenging ideas do not work out in the end because they are too complicated to follow.

Managers and Leaders in a Nonprofit Organization

To a lot of people, the title of manager is closely allied to a leader. Managers are frequently in a position in an organization where they have the power to oversee others, as well as decide on the guiding principles. Although a manager in a nonprofit organization may be seen as a leader, it does not necessarily signify he or she has good leadership skills. Kotter (1990) reported that contemporary administration deals mainly with planning and financial planning, systematizing and recruitment, controlling, and keeping an eye on the organization. A leader creates a feeling of direction by developing a vision of the future. A leader also must communicate with the workers, supporting cooperation, inspiring, and encouraging the workers, in turn, to commit to the company's objectives (Kotter 1990). This signifies that a particular person may well be a manager devoid of being a leader or a leader devoid of being a manager.

Bennis and Nanus and Zaleznik (as cited in Yukl 2006) made the case that leadership and management are jointly exclusive; management and leadership cannot reside within the same individual. A few are managers, and a few are leaders. The differences in the two are made known within the definition they create. A manager seeks stability, sequence, and effectiveness. At the same time, leaders seek suppleness, novelty, and variety (Yukl 2006). When carrying it to the extreme, it is evident the two terminologies may not coexist within the same individual. The majority of researchers have the same opinion though that although they view being in the lead and managing in the role of different procedures, a leader and a manager may perhaps be the same individual (Yukl 2006). Hughes, Ginnet, and Curphy (2006) formulated a clear picture.

Hughes et al. (2006) agreed guidance and management are two partly overlapping roles. Their point of view is that management is linked by an individual's bureaucratic everyday jobs and responsibilities, which come with possessing a particular position inside an establishment. Hence, leadership is linked to the manager who has sway and inspires the workers, in turn, to accomplish the objectives of the establishment. Toor and Ofori (2008) suggested managers must enhance their leadership skills. To achieve this, organizations need to add methods that aid in growing their managers into persons who know how to lead. Capowski (1994) also had the same opinion that improved leadership and management are compulsory, as well as that more leadership is required.

A STUDY OF MANAGEMENT LEADERSHIP QUALITIES WITHIN A NONPROFIT HUMAN SERVICE ORGANIZATION

The role of the manager in a nonprofit organization

Managers are summoned upon to demonstrate the quality of leadership and a leader the skills to manage in a tricky state of affairs. Repeatedly, managers are depicted as a methodological bureaucrat or manager, a person within an establishment with documented power, whose tactics put in order, as well as put into operation, the presented directions of the establishment (Koontz and Weihrich 1986). The function of the supervisor necessitates flexibility, strength, management skills, and leadership attributes. A manager's workings are multifaceted and multidimensional. There are specific skills needed to manage an organization. Primarily, the critical roles of a manager involve planning, putting in order, controlling; and in turn, to efficiently accomplish these functions, specific skills are obtained along with a division of duties among employees. Katz (1974) defined *skill* as "an ability which can be developed, not necessarily inborn, and which are manifested in performance, not merely in potential" (p. 49). Thus, the principal criterion of skillfulness is effective action under varying conditions.

Nonprofit organizations are a broad conception that may be understood in a different way by different persons and, hence, may be difficult to identify. Present are a number of kinds, both within the public and private segment, that are talked about in the literature concerning nonprofit organizations. Although the universal meaning of a *nonprofit organization* is that it works with no profitable function, it is significant that the potential profit will be reinvested within the organization and benefit the employees.

Morris, Kuratho, and Covin (2008) described a nonprofit organization as a kind of establishment that can be of all magnitudes and characteristically serve a societal intention or civic benefit and does not deal out proceeds to shareholders. The nonprofit segment consists of a broad scope of organizations serving different intentions. The diverse kinds of nonprofit organizations may be classified into three all-purpose groups (Morris et al. 2008). The task of the nonprofit organization is to create public value rather than generate profit, and their objectives are frequently not as transparent and well-defined as in commercial organizations. Further, their administration may not be as practiced and accomplished as in organizations with a for-profit intention (Morris et al. 2008).

Nonprofit organizations are organized differently from for-profit organizations. The reason being is not for these organizations to make a profit but instead to work using donations, government funding, and private funding to help aid people who may not receive the services they need. Therefore, the focus of organizations is not what approaches they use to make money, however, finding ways to do fundraising so the quality of services offered on a limited budget is high and aids as many people as possible. Donations are sometimes given to nonprofit companies; then again, the sums given do not lead to the purchasing of extra services for the clients. Typically, the donations help cover administrative costs, and the amount contributed needs to be accounted for. Administrative costs are required to organize services and safeguard the successful operation of the company. Then how do contributors determine the money they are giving is well spent?

Nonprofit organizations are exposed to more rules with respects to how their funding is spent than for-profit companies (Carney 2001). One such rule is that an organization cannot use more than 14 percent of funds given by the government for administrative costs ("Department of Human Services, Dane County" 2008). This means if a person needed ten thousand dollars from the government to purchase services for a human service organization, no extra funds other than one thousand four hundred dollars might be spent on case management, office rentals, and office supplies. It appears suitable and ethical for this sort of rule to exist in not-for-profit organizations since it helps to safeguard that managers are not overpaid and that clients are getting the services they need.

Making available funding to organizations that assist people in the community benefits a vast number of people. To begin with, it benefits the actual individuals receiving services because they are able to live on their own and have more autonomy and influence over what happens in their daily lives. It also helps the community and taxpayers since the funding the government provides comes from taxpayers.

In 2007, Tim Truitt published a dissertation entitled "Exploring Effects of Innovation Management: A Selective Study of Nonprofit Manager Perceptions." The dissertation was completed at Northcentral University—Graduate School of Business and Technology Management.

Truitt conducted a qualitative manifold unit case study on the observations of managers at eight nonprofit organizations situated in the United States, New Zealand, and Europe regarding management techniques as tools for fostering innovation (Truitt 2007). Information was collected using in-depth interviews. Significant findings demonstrated that resources used by managers to promote modernism were the use of technology and incentive programs.

The difficulty is that the information about the best practices to make it easy for innovation in the nonprofit organization was apparent, but the organization did not have significant research to demonstrate they used the best methods. The reason for this study was to summarize and explain how managers at nonprofit organizations could generate situations that promote innovation. These depictions can offer relevant information for nonprofit organizations hoping to benefit from innovation for upcoming researchers who are studying the leaders of organizations to comprehend what they need to know to create an atmosphere conducive to innovation. (Truitt 2007). The research questions were (a) what approaches do managers of nonprofit organizations put into practice to promote innovation? (b) What supplies do managers of nonprofit organizations provide to advance innovation? The writer also listed two copied research proposals: (a) quality management and empowerment methods are apparent by managers of nonprofit organizations as being helpful tools for endorsing modernism, and (b) organizational procedures (mainly teambuilding and planned organization) are apparent by managers of nonprofit organizations as useful tools for advocating innovation (Truitt 2007).

The problem statement, purpose statement, and research questions are all in agreement. Their objective is to decide if perceptions of making innovation are correct and the research queries examine the plan and resources managers are utilizing to make this innovation.

The approach applied in this research was a case study. The person behind this study found eight unique organizations (Truitt 2007). He interviewed one delegate from every one of these organization in depth to obtain background information on the organizations and to become familiar with the perceptions of an important figure within each individual company.

He discovered the major limitations of this study were with the case study method; his results were not entirely transferable for other organizations (Truitt 2007). He utilized eight distinct organizations; therefore, this was not a large enough model to make universal statements about nonprofit organizations. In addition, the model was not sufficiently random. Truitt met with one spokesperson from each company and determined there may be respondent biases: also, his study did not produce quantitative data that could be used to strengthen observed associations.

The inferences of his study were that the outcomes might give helpful direction for other organizations in the nonprofit field. He did not believe all information obtained from the interviews could be pertinent to other companies, but the outcomes could present suggestions or new plan ideas for other organizations. The recommendations for future study are to do more quantitative work to validate the answers of the case studies and to do more qualitative work to help make outcomes more simplifiable (Truitt 2007).

The recognized limitations, inferences, and suggestions are reliable with case study research since the number of contributors is small. When there are few contributors, the capacity to generalize the findings to the majority is diminished.

Organizational Culture

Organizational culture is a discipline of study that examines how employees work together within an organization. The culture of an organization frequently describes how the organization will do business and make its products or services. *Culture* could be identified as an organization's fundamental beliefs and assumptions regarding what the company is about, how the members should behave, and how it is identified in relation to the external environment (Morris et al. 2008). Morris et al. (2008) argued it is essential for organizations to have a clearly identified culture to create a sustainable entrepreneurial spirit within the organization. Within the human service field, manufactured goods are not sold; but to a certain extent, a service is made available to people with disabilities, families who need extra support, persons with mental illness, and persons with drug and alcohol dependence. The background of the organizations that offer these services is frequently distinct from a company that creates a product to be sold since these companies spend a significant quantity of time with a client who attains services from the organization.

Perceptions of Leadership and Management

The success of leaders depends upon how their employees identify them. A key player in the employee-organization relationship is the manager. Management represents the organization in the eyes of the employees. Trevino and Nelson (2011) noted the representative nature of management stating, "Managers are the lens through which employees view the organization too many employees, managers are the organization" (p. 36). Serving as credible agents of the organization (Eisenberger et al. 2010), managers personify or embody the organization (Sluss et al. 2012). When looking at most aspects of the organization-employee relationship, managers play a unique and distinct role in spanning the boundary. As a consequence, employees' perceptions of their direct managers and indirect managers within the organization become increasingly important to the success and sustainability of the organization. The following sections review various authors' studies and understandings of how subordinates identify their managers.

Holloway (2012) performed an experiential study with the hypothesis that task-oriented and relationship-oriented leadership behaviors are allied to the workers' perceptions of organizational climate. The vital significance of the study was in the notion that workers are potentially of uppermost importance within the organizations. The study realms of leadership and organizational climate are completely linked. The analysis examined the following research question: are task-oriented and relationship-oriented leadership behaviors allied to different sizes of organizational climate within a nonprofit organization? The methodology was an amalgam of two quantitative catalysts, a web-based survey consisting of seventy-nine inquiries intended to determine the comparative input to task-oriented and relationship-oriented leadership behaviors. The outcomes of the study demonstrated particular leadership activities have an effect on a small number of dimensions of organizational climate. The investigation also discovered task-oriented leadership activities possess a constructive and important relationship with the warmness of the organizational climate dimension.

Mohamed and Nguyen (2011) conducted an empirical study to examine the connection between leadership behaviors and management information. The authors' plan was to examine the influence of transformational and transactional leadership behaviors on knowledge management in organizations screening effects of organizational culture on this correlation, in the context of small to medium-sized companies operating in Australia. Four hypotheses were planned for testing. It provided a concise evaluation of knowledge management fundamentals pertinent to the study, the association between management and knowledge management and management and organizational culture. This was a useful study because the outcome showed convincing evidence in support of the moderating role of managerial culture on the association between transactional leadership and knowledge management.

Glisson (1978) performed a study with path psychoanalysis of data from thirty human service organizations. The outcome supports the requirement of technological standardization in dependent associations with four variables. This was supported on the basis it focused on one method. This analysis showed both management's and subordinates' views in the human service field, which is significant for contrast purposes to studies conducted in other types of organizations.

A STUDY OF MANAGEMENT LEADERSHIP QUALITIES WITHIN A NONPROFIT HUMAN SERVICE ORGANIZATION

Brotheridge and Long (2007) discussed the everyday problems supervisors deal with and the means and answers available to supervisors. The authors assumed supervisors were conscious of their means and capability to find answers to problems. The reasons of the study were "to examine the day-to-day problems that managers face in trying to be effective and the resources and solutions that they access as means of dealing with these challenges" (Brotheridge and Long 2007, 10). The authors achieved their objective and established that the solution to the research question was useful information comes from the people around them instead of from point sources, and the supervisors were not likely to view experts as sources of help.

Harel and Conen (1982) discussed expectation theory in regard to professional obsolescence in the workplace because it is becoming a growing concern for supervisors and organizations. This matter influences not only the value of work but also the way workers are viewed by management. The researchers used expectancy theory to study professional obsolescence.

Abdel-Halim (1979) performed a study to assess the experience of power between the managers and their employees. Facts were acquired from a model of 222 supervisory and nonsupervisory employees in five hierarchical rankings. The researcher wrote about the conventional and innovative paradigms because this included studying various levels. This was a fascinating study because it involved employees and managers from different positions and levels, which show if perceptions are comparable across all areas or if they vary.

Bloom, Parlette, and O'Reilly disputed that nurses are looking for independence and control within their workplace. Alternatively, managers believe nurses should eagerly do what they are instructed. This difference in perception is an interesting feature of how this topic has been examined, and it offers some insight in bringing employee perceptions and organizational perceptions closer together. This was written based on the grounds of the paradigm view since the author approached the subject with the idea that there was one right answer. Investigating the perceptions of nurses and their managers is useful for understanding the broader topic of management perceptions; however, perceptions may vary in other types of organizations.

Conclusion

In summary, a subordinate most likely would want to work with a manager who utilizes the situational management style instead of the authoritative management style since more importance is given to the employees. Of all the management methods, the transformational management style is the greatest since it demonstrates a significant concern for both employees and for finishing the task.

In an attempt to advance organizational culture and behavior, particularly managers' and subordinates' perceptions and their effects, a literature review has been performed. The subjects and results of these articles were evaluated. Restrictions, inferences, and suggestions were evaluated, demonstrating that even though a number of articles have been written that touch on managers' insights, the subject can be improved, and there is a need for more research on the subject (Lindberg 1999), particularly in this region of examination.

The information obtained in this literature review demonstrates many organizations are undergoing various perceptions among managers and workers. This is noteworthy to record since the dissimilarity may give details about why some organizations have difficulty with motivation and leadership.

This literature review provides an analysis of information sources of leadership in the human service field. This was a multifaceted study since it included the dynamics of human service organizations, which are distinctive from corporate industries since they concentrate on the value of services offered and the welfare of the people who obtain services. It was not centered on creating profit but instead on the bettering of persons and the populations in which they live. It also included the leadership abilities of supervisors who had dual roles within an organization and the perceptions of their employees.

Chapter 3: Methodology

Introduction

This chapter explains the process of data collection. It is divided into ten sections followed by a summary. The first section describes the design of the study and includes the research questions and a description of the survey. The second and third sections describe the population of interest and sample derived from it. The fourth, fifth, and sixth sections describe variables and test factors. The seventh section describes steps taken to establish data validity and how reliability was measured after the data were collected. The eighth and ninth sections describe the data collection procedures and coding and specify the data analysis plan, respectively. The final and tenth section addresses research ethics and protection of subjects. The chapter ends with a summary.

Design of the Study

This was a quantitative, nonexperimental, exploratory study. Its design was a two-group comparison. The two groups were comprised of managers working at a nonprofit human services organization and distinguished by the presence or absence of a human services degree.

Three research questions guided the study. Data were collected with a survey.

Research Questions

Three research questions guided this study. They are listed below with the corresponding hypotheses.

RQ 1: Is there a difference in objectives or goals emphasis, as a leadership behavior, between nonprofit human services managers with and without human service degrees?

$H_0$1: The difference in objectives or goals emphasis between nonprofit human services managers with and without human service degrees is not statistically significant.

H_A1: Nonprofit human services managers with human service degrees put significantly more emphasis on objectives or goals than do managers without human service degrees.

RQ 2: Is there a difference in personal support, as a leadership behavior, between nonprofit human services managers with and without human service degrees?

$H_0$2: The difference in personal support between nonprofit human services managers with and without human service degrees is not statistically significant.

H_A2: Nonprofit human services managers with human service degrees put significantly less emphasis on personal support than do managers without human service degrees.

RQ 3: Is there a difference in work easing, as a leadership behavior, between nonprofit human services managers with and without human service degrees?

$H_0$3: The difference in work easing between nonprofit human services managers with and without human service degrees is not statistically significant.

H_A3: Nonprofit human services managers with human service degrees put significantly more emphasis on work easing than do managers without human service degrees.

A STUDY OF MANAGEMENT LEADERSHIP QUALITIES WITHIN A NONPROFIT HUMAN SERVICE ORGANIZATION

Data Collection Instrument: The Nonprofit Organizational Leadership Survey

Data were collected with the nonprofit organizational leadership survey shown in Table 1. It is comprised of twenty closed-ended survey items. The first five items solicit general demographic information. Items six through nine solicit general information from the participant about their manager's background, effectiveness, and experience with the manager. Items 10–18 use a seven-point Likert scale of agreement (1 = strongly disagree, 2 = disagree, 3 = slightly disagree, 4 = neither agree nor disagree, 5 = slightly agree, 6 = agree, and 7 = strongly agree) with statements pertaining to the three leadership behaviors of interest in this study (objectives or goals emphasis, personal support, and work easing or facilitation). The numeric values of the response array are such that the higher values reflect significant agreement. Items 19 and 20 solicit opinions on the ideal leadership style for nonprofit organizations.

Items 10–18 on Table 1 were drawn from the well-validated leadership survey, the Michigan Assessment of Organizations (MAO; University of Michigan, Survey Research Center 1975). The complete MAO has ten modules; items 10–18 in the current study (see Table 1) were derived from module 6, "Supervising Behavior," which examines the ways the employees perceive supervisors by obtaining descriptions of competence, style, and general leadership behavior.

Research Instrument

Leadership—Michigan Organizational Assessment Survey

Please fill in general demographic information

Item	Survey Item
1	What is your gender? Male Female
2	How old are you? _____ years
3	What is your race? _____
4	What is your marital status? _____

DR. SHARON REED

5. How many years have you been working with your current organization? _____ years

Please select the one that best describes your perceptions of your immediate leader or manager

When answering the following questions, please think about your immediate leader or manager.

6. Manager's educational background: human services degree; degree other than human services degree; no degree I am aware of

7. Manager's professional background: human services background; background in something other than human services

8. How effective is your manager? Pleases choose one number between 1 and 10, with 1 = not at all effective, 10 = maximally effective.

9. How many years have you been working with this manager? _____ years

10	Help subordinates with personal problems	SD	D	SLD	N	SLA	A	SA
11	Make sure subordinates have clear goals to achieve	SD	D	SLD	N	SLA	A	SA
12	Keep subordinates informed about the work which is being done	SD	D	SLD	N	SLA	A	SA
13	Make sure subordinates know what has to be done	SD	D	SLD	N	SLA	A	SA
14	Be concerned about subordinates as people	SD	D	SLD	N	SLA	A	SA
15	Make it clear how subordinates should do their jobs	SD	D	SLD	N	SLA	A	SA
16	Help subordinates discover problems before they get too bad	SD	D	SLD	N	SLA	A	SA
17	Feel each subordinate is important as an individual	SD	D	SLD	N	SLA	A	SA

| 18 | Help them solve work-related problems | SD | D | SLD | N | SLA | A | SA |

19 In your opinion, what is the ideal leadership style for a nonprofit human services manager? Please choose one of the following.

Authoritarian: leaders who have an authoritarian management style have a high concern for task and little concern for people.

Compromise management: Leaders who have a compromise management style have a moderate concern for tasks and a moderate concern for people. This kind of manager attempts to stabilize the importance of completing the task while connecting to the subordinates and keeping them pleased since the team is usually effective and they get along with the manager. Compromise managers are capable of eliciting respect from subordinates because they listen to and incorporate subordinates' ideas.

Transformational leadership: Leaders who have a transformational management style are involved with feelings, morals, values, and long-term goals.

Situational leadership: Leaders who have a situational leadership management style are rooted in the communication among the sizes of relationship activities and task activities, in addition to employees' willingness or maturity in favor of performing a particular task.

20 Which leadership style is the best for a nonprofit organization? Authoritarian, compromise management, transformational leadership, situational leadership

Note. SD = Strongly Disagree (value = 1), D = Disagree; SLD = Slightly Disagree; N = Neither Agree nor Disagree, SLA = Slightly Agree, A = Agree, SA = Strongly Agree (value = 7)

Population

The population of interest was comprised of direct-care employees who worked in the field of nonprofit human services in the United States. Their duties involved providing direct care to residential individuals with physical, psychological, acquired, developmental disabilities.

Sample

The assessable sample was a nonprofit human services organization in Massachusetts with 500 employees that agreed to allow me to invite their employees to participate via dissemination of the survey (see Table 1) via an e-mail link (see section on data collection procedure). Employees of this organization provided direct residential, work-related, and transportation services to individuals with acquired brain injuries and other psychological, bodily, acquired, or developmental disabilities. Consequently, they reflected the population of interest. Most of these employees had managers although some had the dual role of director and employee manager.

Dependent Variables

A dependent variable changes when exposed to one or more influential factors (Creswell 2003). There were three dependent variables in the current study. Each corresponded to one of the nonprofit human services manager's leadership behaviors: objectives or goals emphasis, personal support, or work easing. These three leadership behaviors were measured and examined to determine if they varied in relation to the nonprofit human services managers' degree of education.

Independent Variable

An independent variable is an influential factor that occurs separately from the behaviors or attitudes it influences (Creswell 2003). In the current study, the independent variable was the type of degree. It had two levels (yes, the manager held a human service degree; no, the manager did not hold a human service degree). That is, nonprofit human services managers' degree of education was the variable predicted to influence the extent to which managers emphasized objectives or goals, personal support, and work easing or facilitation.

Test Factors

Demographic data (i.e., gender, age, ethnicity, marital status, and time with the organization; see Table 1) were examined to ascertain if they served as influential secondary factors that affected participants' perceptions of their managers. That is, these variables were examined to determine if they were significant covariates with perceptions about managers collected using the MAO (see Table 1).

Reliability and Validity

A useful study is both valid and reliable (Creswell 2003). A study that is reliable because it was based on a consistent measurement instrument is of no value, if not valid, because the instrument could not provide data useful for answering the research question. Alternatively, a study that is valid because it was based on a measurement instrument that provided useful data for answering the research question is of no value if the results are unreliable because of flawed application of the data collection instrument.

Validity refers to the accurate and precise outcomes of a study because the data collected were the type of data needed to answer the research questions accurately and precisely (Humbley and Zumbo 1996). Two kinds of validity should be ensured throughout the research procedure: internal validity and exterior validity (Campbell and Stanley 1963). Internal validity makes certain the basic necessities for the research have been met to produce accurate results. Threats to internal validity can involve events during data collection that could influence perceptions (e.g., perceptions of employees taking the survey about their managers could be altered by accusations of sexual abuse of female employees by male managers of nonprofit human services organizations broadcast across national media); dissimilarities across testing environments, instruments, or participant selection; statistical regression; and maturation. These threats were minimized in the current study in two ways: by sampling direct-care employees in one large Massachusetts nonprofit human services organization (with 500 employees) that was wholly consistent with the type of working environment pertinent to answering this study's research questions about managers and across a brief period of two to three weeks.

Exterior validity questions whether the results of a study would be oversimplified or otherwise inapplicable to other settings. External validity was pertinent to the current study because a broader goal was to obtain evidence of the relationship between manager leadership behaviors and education that could be of practical utility to all nonprofit human services organizations that match the one used in the current study (i.e., not just reflective of the specific Massachusetts facility used to sample employee perceptions). The threat to exterior validity includes overfitting the data to the specific Massachusetts facility used to sample employee perceptions—i.e., contact influence of testing (Campbell and Stanley 1963). This threat was minimized by collecting a large sample that was broadly representative of the employees of nonprofit human services organizations.

The reliability of the data was further assumed because it was based on the well-established and long-term reliability of the MAO survey instrument (University of Michigan, Survey Research Center 1975). Otherwise, the survey used in the current study was developed by the principal investigator and had not been formally validated psychometrically. Instead, the data's internal consistency or reliability were evaluated in two ways. One, the consistency of answers to individual survey statements was examined with visual inspection of descriptive statistics for each variable. Two, conceptually similar survey items were grouped and their overall internal consistency evaluated with Cronbach's α (Gliner and Morgan 2000). Cronbach's α is used for surveys that include a number of conceptually related statements measured on Likert or dichotomous scales only administrated once. Cronbach's α is a commonly employed test of internal consistency that views each statement within each set of conceptually related statements as a retest of another item. In essence, Cronbach's formula generates all possible test-retest pairs of correlations and provides the mean as the reliability index α, which ranges in value from 0 to 1. The closer Cronbach's α is to one, the higher the reliability of the database. Indices of .70 or higher reflect an adequately reliable database.

Data Collection Procedure and Coding

E-mailing the link to an online survey is an efficient and cost-effective way to distribute surveys to a large number of potential participants (Boneva, Kraut, and Froehlich 2001). Once the institutional review board (IRB) permission to conduct the current study was obtained, the Nonprofit Organizational Leadership Survey (see Table 1) was uploaded to the online survey website SurveyMonkey. Then an e-mail message inviting employees of the Massachusetts nonprofit human services organization to participate in this study (see Appendix A), and including the link to the online survey, was e-mailed to the organization's director. The director agreed to send the invitational e-mail to employees *en masse* once per week for a three-week period, encouraging them to complete the survey.

There were possible 500 potential participants. A power analysis conducted on the GPower website calculated a minimum of $N = 102$ participants to find a medium effect (Cohen's $d = .50$) at .80 power and $\alpha = .05$ of a two-group comparison. The survey remained open for 3 weeks or until $N = 102$ participants were obtained, whichever came first. However, the goal was to obtain 200–300 participants from the facility for greater representativeness and generalizability.

Once the data were downloaded from SurveyMonkey, identifying information was replaced by case numbers. The information given by the participants through the survey stayed confidential. The data were kept in a password-secured computer available only to the researcher. No one had access to the computer unless subpoenaed by a court.

Data were coded by educational group (yes, held a human service degree; no, did not hold a human service degree) with a nominal variable. Gender, ethnicity, marital status, managers' professional background, and the ideal leadership style of nonprofit managers and nonprofit organizations were also coded as nominal data. Remaining variables were coded as continuous or ratio-scaled data.

Data Analysis Plan

The data were analyzed with SPSS v 25 dedicated statistical software. First, the data were screened for statistical normality. Second, reliability statistics were conducted (Cronbach's α on conceptually similar survey items). Third, summated scaled scores were generated for the three leadership behaviors of interest (aims emphasis, personal support, and work easing). Demographic variables were then summarized to characterize the modal participant. Correlations were inspected to look for covariates and sufficient correlations among dependent variables to establish whether analysis of covariance (ANCOVA), multivariate analysis of variance (MANOVA), or multivariate analysis of covariance (MANCOVA) tests were justified. In the absence of covariates, RQs 1–3 were analyzed with independent *t*-tests. In the presence of covariates, RQs 1–3 were analyzed with one-by-two ANCOVA tests. The dependent variables (leadership behaviors: aims emphasis, personal support, and work easing) were sufficiently correlated; MANOVA tests were used. In the presence of covariates, MANCOVA testes were used. Statistical significance was set at $\alpha = .05$.

Research Ethics and Protection of Subjects

The primary ethical matter of conducting a study with a survey is to ensure information collected stays confidential (Beauchamp 2003). Moreover, participants are most likely to respond accurately to a survey when they trust that their responses will remain anonymous (Gliner and Morgan 2000). The current study involved an important but potentially challenging topic: the behavior of supervisors. Therefore, *confidentiality*, defined as guidelines that restrict certain kinds of information, took priority. Confidentiality was maintained by replacing any identifying information with a case number. Additionally, data remained on a password-protected computer; the only person with access to that computer's password was the researcher. All data will be shredded three years after the completion of the study. Each participant was informed that his or her participation was voluntary and of their right to withdraw without penalty at any time.

Consent form

The first page of the survey was the "Informed Consent to Participate in Research" consent form (Appendix B) to obtain participant consent before taking the survey. The consent form, set forth in language both accessible to and understandable by participants, explained the purpose of the survey, the volunteer nature of participation, procedures that protect their confidentiality, rights to decline to answer any questions or finish the survey, and that they would not receive any compensation. Participants were asked to agree to the consent form before data collection began.

Limitations

Limitations are inherent elements in the research that can influence the researcher's ability to obtain accurate results but that the researcher cannot control (Gliner and Morgan 2000). Limitations in the current study included employees' willingness to participate, lack of external verification that they were human services employees, and that they worked for the manager they evaluated on the survey. Another limitation over, which the researcher had no control, was an employee's potentially unique exposure to ethical dilemmas regarding managers in human services settings.

This study generated self-report data, which were artificial to some extent because they did not directly measure participants' behavior in the environment where the behavior typically occurred and were frequently influenced by participants' awareness that they were being studied and/or wished to appear socially desirable to the researcher, a limitation known as social desirability bias (Gliner and Morgan 2000). Along these lines, another limitation was that participants may have wished to conceal something, acted on the need to "cover" for what they believed to be their managers' or their own shortcomings, or erred on the side of "the professional response" (e.g., our facility is fully operational in every way, including manager expertise). Untested assumptions of this research are that participants were candid and communicated their manager's behavior honestly.

Delimitations

The primary delimitation was that participants were current employees of a nonprofit human services organization working in the northeastern United States (rather than other regions of the United States).

Summary

The purpose of the research was to identify the extent to which employees in nonprofit human services organizations perceived their managers exhibit three types of leadership behaviors (aims emphasis, personal support, and work easing) and determine if these leadership behaviors varied by formal manager education in human services. This was a quantitative, nonexperimental, exploratory study. Its design was a two-group comparison; the two groups were comprised of managers working at a nonprofit human services organization who were distinguished by the presence or absence of a human services degree. Three research questions guided this study.

RQ 1: Is there a difference in aims emphasis, as a leadership behavior, between nonprofit human services managers with and without human service degrees?

RQ 2: Is there a difference in personal support, as a leadership behavior, between nonprofit human services managers with and without human service degrees?

RQ 3: Is there a difference in work easing, as a leadership behavior, between nonprofit human services managers with and without human service degrees?

A STUDY OF MANAGEMENT LEADERSHIP QUALITIES WITHIN A NONPROFIT HUMAN SERVICE ORGANIZATION

Data were collected with the Nonprofit Organizational Leadership Survey. The population of interest was comprised of employees who worked in the field of nonprofit human services in the United States. The quantifiable sample was a nonprofit human services organization in Massachusetts with 500 employees. There were three dependent variables in the current study, each a manager leadership behavior: aims emphasis, personal support, and work easing. The independent variable was the type of degree (with two levels: yes, the manager held a human service degree; no, the manager did not hold a human service degree). Variables were examined to determine if they were significant covariates. Threats to internal validity were minimized by sampling employees in one large Massachusetts nonprofit human services organization that was wholly consistent with the type of working environment pertinent to answering this study's research questions about managers and across a brief period of two to three weeks. The threat to external validity was minimized by collecting a large sample that was broadly representative of the employees of nonprofit human services organizations. Data were collected via an online survey by an invitational e-mail sent to employees by the facility director once per week for 3 weeks or until 102 participants were generated. The two-group analysis used t-tests, analysis of variance (ANOVA), ANCOVA, MANOVA, or MANCOVA tests depending on the relationship among the variables.

Chapter 4: Results

The purpose of this research was to study employee perspectives on the leadership style of managers within nonprofit institutions. Specifically, this study intended to understand the effects of leadership style on employees in human services organizations located in the northeastern United States. The study was a two-group design. Two groups of employees were compared on the quality of leadership between their managers, differentiated by managers who held human services degrees and managers who did not hold human services degrees. Quality of leadership was measured as three specific leadership behaviors (objectives or goals emphasis, personal support, and work easing or facilitation). The intent was to identify management factors that could improve the functioning of a human services organization.

This results chapter is divided into seven sections. The first section lists the research questions. The second section briefly describes data screening, reliability, summated scales, and statistical tests used to analyze the data. The third section presents the participants' demographic characteristics. The fourth section presents descriptive statistics for summated scales and managerial effectiveness, along with correlations for identifying the analytical approach to address the research questions. The fifth section presents the results of research questions 1, 2, and 3. The sixth section presents participant perspectives on ideal nonprofit leadership. The seventh and final section is the summary.

Research Questions

This study was guided by three research questions. They correspond to the three leadership behaviors of interest (objectives or goals emphasis, personal support, and work easing or facilitation). Associated hypotheses are listed in sections that present the results for the research questions.

RQ 1: Is there a difference in objectives or goals emphasis, as a leadership behavior, between nonprofit human services managers with and without human services degrees?

RQ 2: Is there a difference in personal support, as a leadership behavior, between nonprofit human services managers with and without human services degrees?

RQ 3: Is there a difference in work easing or facilitation, as a leadership behavior, between nonprofit human services managers with and without human services degrees?

Data Screening, Reliability, Summated Scales, and Statistical Tests

This section briefly describes data screening, testing the reliability or internal consistency of the data, generating summated scales and statistical tests used to analyze the data. Statistical tests were χ^2s, correlations, and MANCOVA.

Data screening

All data were initially screened for entry errors and missing data points. The data were collected on the online survey site SurveyMonkey, so there were no entry errors. There was a small number of missing data points; but these did not show any systematic pattern, although the number of participants in various analyses (Ns) tended to vary slightly. Likert-scaled responses were screened for normality, linearity, homoscedasticity, and outliers to determine if they could be treated as continuous data (Hair et al. 2010). Following Warner (2013), the decision was made ahead of time to retain outliers because they reflect the practical reality of human services organizations, and the goal of this research was to understand the reality of human services organizations better. Low scores emerged as low outliers in all three leadership behaviors of interest (i.e., objectives or goals emphasis, personal support, and work easing or facilitation as described below), but the data did not otherwise show any substantial departures from statistical normality. Therefore, Likert-scaled data were treated as continuous data and examined with parametric inferential statistical tests to examine group differences.

Percentages were rounded off to whole numbers and may not add up to precisely 100%. Data were analyzed with SPSS v 25, which is dedicated statistical software. Statistical significance was set at $\alpha = .05$.

Reliability

Reliability statistics (i.e., internal consistency) were conducted on conceptually similar survey items with Cronbach's α for the three leadership behaviors of interest (i.e., objectives or goals emphasis, personal support, and work easing or facilitation). Cronbach's α statistics range in value from 0 to 1. The closer Cronbach's α is to 1, the higher the reliability of the database. Indices of .70 or higher reflect an adequately reliable database (Gliner and Morgan 2000).

Summated scale scores

A summated scale was generated for each of the three leadership behaviors of interest (objectives or goals emphasis, personal support, and work easing or facilitation). A summated scale is a single empirical measure that represents multiple aspects of a construct in one variable (Hair et al. 2010). Deriving a single measure from several related aspects decreases the measurement error in the original data points, which increases data reliability and validity, as well as parsimony in the overall number of variables (Hair et al. 2010). Because each summated score was a mean, its possible values ranged from 1 to

7 (1 = strongly disagree, 7 = strongly agree) like the Likert scale used to measure responses to survey items.

Aims emphasis. Two survey items measured the leadership dimension of aims emphasis. An example of a survey item that measured aims emphasis is, "My manager makes sure subordinates have clear goals to achieve." Internal consistency was high, Cronbach's α = .74. Because of high internal consistency, a summated scale (SS) was generated, using the mean response of the related items. It is hereafter called the aims emphasis SS.

Personal support. Three survey items measured the leadership dimension of personal support. An example of a survey item that measured personal support is, "My manager is concerned about his or her subordinates as people." Cronbach's α showed that internal consistency was high, α = .84. Because of high internal consistency, a summated scale (SS) was generated, using the mean response of the related items. It is hereafter called the personal support SS.

Work easing. Four items measured the leadership dimension of work easing. An example of a survey item that measured work easing is, "My manager helps his or her subordinates solve work-related problems." Cronbach's α showed that internal consistency was high, α = .94. Because of high internal consistency, a summated scale (SS) was generated, using the mean response of the related items. It is hereafter called the work easing SS.

Chi-square test of independence

A χ^2 test of independence was used to examine demographic variables pertaining to managers' backgrounds in human services and choices for ideal leadership styles. Chi-square tests set up categorical data in cross-tabulated tables. Data were analyzed by comparing the actual number of participants in the database who fell into a specific category (observed frequencies or counts) to the number of participants who would be expected by chance—expected frequencies or counts (Siegel and Castellan 1988). The Yates correction was applied because the data formed a two-by-two table, and the correction reduced the observed-expected difference by half a point so that it fit χ^2 distributions more accurately. The overall χ^2 statistic indicates whether the observed counts differ significantly or nonsignificantly from counts expected by chance. For significant χ^2 statistics, individual pairs of observed and expected frequencies are then inspected for statistical significance by transforming observed/expected differences into z scores called *adjusted residuals*. Statistically significant relationships are revealed by adjusted residuals that are ± 1.96 (Siegel and Castellan 1988).

Correlations

Pearson product-moment correlations were used to examine the data for covariates. Phi (Φ) and Cramer's V correlations were used to measure the strength of relationships between categorical variables in χ^2s. All were interpreted categorically following Cohen (1988, 79–81): small effect $r = .10$, medium effect $r = .30$, large effect $r = .50$. It is generally recommended that sample sizes be at least $N = 100$ when correlations are used, partly to have adequate statistical power and partly to minimize the effect of extreme outliers (Warner 2013). The dataset in the current study met Warner's criterion.

MANCOVA test

Research questions 1–3 were addressed with a version of the MANOVA test called a MANCOVA. Like all ANOVA tests, this test is designed to determine the statistical significance of group differences (Hair et al. 2010). However, different from ANOVA tests, MANOVA tests are multivariate tests that examine two or more related dependent variables simultaneously. In the current study, the related dependent variables that were examined simultaneously were the three leadership behaviors of interest (objectives or goals emphasis, personal support, and work easing or facilitation). In contrast, ANOVA tests are univariate tests because each only examines one dependent variable at a time.

MANOVA is preferred over several separate ANOVAs for several reasons (Hair et al. 2010, Warner 2013). Complex phenomena, such as leadership style in human services organizations in the current study, are more accurate when measured in multiple ways because it can be very challenging to obtain accurate measures of a complex phenomenon from a single measure of it. MANOVA results can be more informative than a series of univariate ANOVA tests because MANOVA takes intercorrelations among the dependent variables into account by treating them in combination. The MANOVA calculations create a new dependent variable that is the linear combination of the original dependent variables, which maximizes group differences; it is called the multivariate dependent variable. The advantage is that a multivariate dependent variable may reveal differences that individual ANOVA tests cannot show. For example, the MANOVA may establish that related dependent variables each represent a conceptually distinct and independent outcome, or intercorrelations suggest they represent multiple measures of one conceptually distinct outcome. Finally, group differences may only emerge when the outcome of two or more dependent variables is considered jointly.

MANOVA yields more output than ANOVA because it is more complex and has up to three steps. In step one, the overall multivariate hypothesis is tested. The most commonly used test statistic to evaluate the significance of this hypothesis is Wilks *lambda* (λ), a measure of the within-groups variance divided by the total variance. The value of λ ranges from zero to one so the smaller the value of λ, the greater the evidence of group differences. If the multivariate null hypothesis is retained, the convention is to stop the analysis at this point and conclude that the intervention (in the current study, whether or not a manager held a human services degree) had no effect (in the current study, on different dimensions of leadership). Effect sizes are measured with partial *Eta* squared (partial η^2), which is the amount of variance in the dependent variable that is explained by the corresponding independent variable, i.e., group membership (Warner 2013).

When the overall multivariate test is statistically significant, step two is to undertake a series of univariate ANOVAs to identify the dependent variable(s) affected by the intervention. A Bonferronilike adjustment is applied to maintain the risk of a type I error at the original α level.

In step three, any univariate test of a dependent variable that results in statistical significance is followed by planned comparisons to identify specific differences with Tukey's tests, when there are more than two levels of the independent variable.

In the current study, research questions 1–3 were addressed with a multivariate analysis of covariance or MANCOVA. MANCOVAs are MANOVAs with the addition of covariates. Covariates are variables that correlate with the dependent variable. The question is whether the covariate influences the dependent variable such that it misleads researchers about differences in the dependent variable from main or interaction effects. MANCOVA first determines if there is a significant covariate effect. If so, it removes the influence of the covariate statistically and then compares the remaining variance in the dependent variable to reveal statistically significant independent variables. In the current study, an overall measure of manager effectiveness was the covariate.

Demographic Characteristics

This section presents the demographic variables and characterizes the modal participant. A total of 113 individuals completed surveys. Of those, 10 participants (cases 4, 14, 20, 21, 33, 45, 62, 78, 101, 105) failed to provide information on their managerial educational background, leadership style, or both. They were eliminated from further analyses, N = 103 participants. The demographic results in this section show that the modal participant was a married Caucasian woman in her 40s who had worked for her current organization for 10 years and for her current manager for 5 years.

There were three times as many participants whose managers did not hold human service degrees, n = 75 participants, 73%, as participants whom managers held human services degrees, n = 28 participants, 28%. The 3:1 ratio of nondegree holders to degree holders is illustrated in Figure 1.

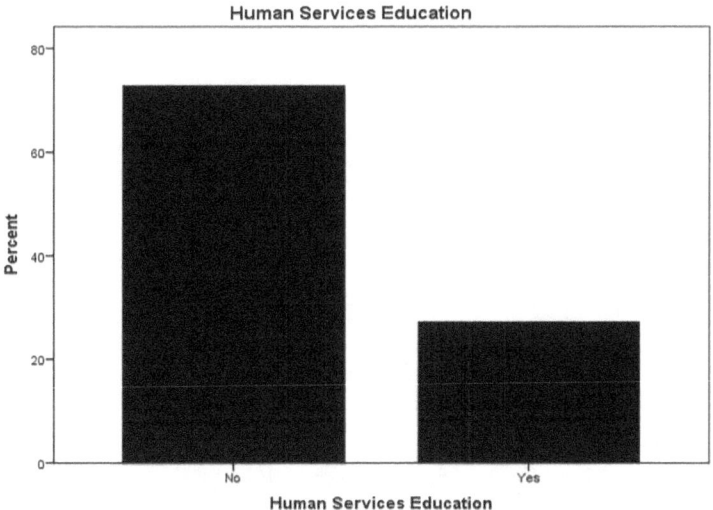

Figure 1. Numbers of participants by human services degrees.

There was a gender ratio of 4-to-1 women to men; women 80%, n = 82 female participants, men 20%, n = 21 male participants. Four of the 103 participants did not provide ethnic information. Of the 99 participants who provided ethnic information, illustrated in Figure 2, the majority of the participants were Caucasian, 77%, n = 76 participants. The next largest group was African American, 12%, n = 12 participants. The remaining ethnicities were each represented by 4 or fewer participants.

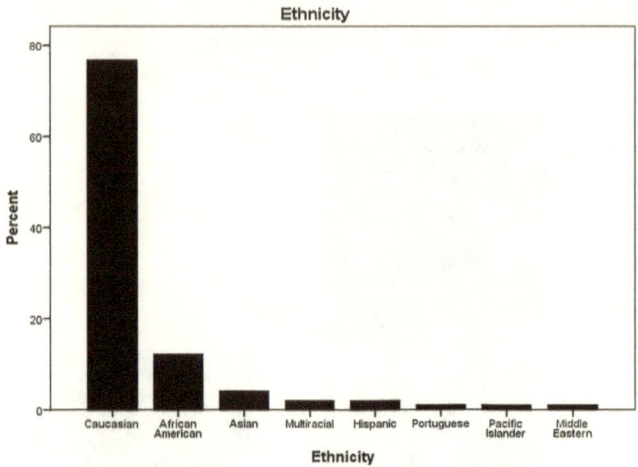

Figure 2. Numbers of participants by ethnicity.

Figure 3 illustrates the participants by marital status. Half were married, 50%, $n = 51$ participants. Approximately half were single, 41%, $n = 42$. Ten participants labeled their marital status as something other than married or single, 10%.

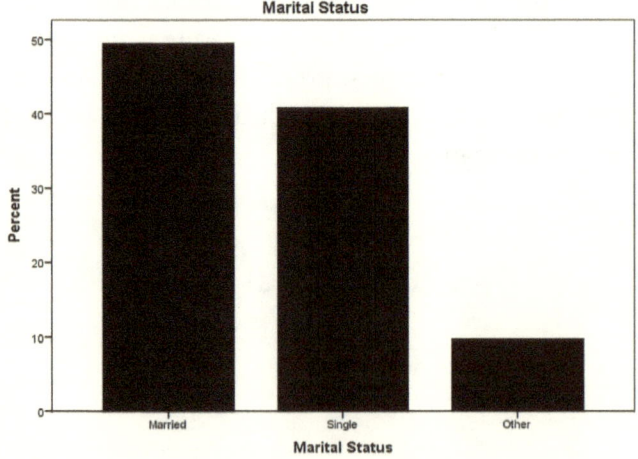

Figure 3. Numbers of participants by marital status.

A STUDY OF MANAGEMENT LEADERSHIP QUALITIES WITHIN A NONPROFIT HUMAN SERVICE ORGANIZATION

Participants were in their early 40s on average, M = 43.38 years old, SD = 13.13 but represented a broad range of ages, *min* = 21 years, *max* = 70 years. They had been working for their current organization nearly 10 years on average, M = 9.84 years, SD = 8.02, though again represented a broad range of time in the current job, *min* = 1 year, *max* = 31 years. They had worked for their current manager about half as long as they had been employed by the organization, M = 4.87 years, SD = 5.48. However, they again reported a broad range, *min* = 1 year, *max* = 30 years.

Each participant was a member of one of two groups: those whose managers held a human services degree and those whose managers did not hold a human services degree. Participants were also asked on the survey whether or not their manager's professional background included human services experience, regardless of formal education.

Figure 4 shows the cross-tabulation of human services degrees (formal education) and professional background (direct experience) among managers. In total, 28 managers held human services degrees. All 28 of them had a professional background in human services as well. The other 74 managers did not hold a human services degree. In a two to one ratio, twice as many nondegree-holding managers had professional backgrounds in human services as did not have professional backgrounds in human services.

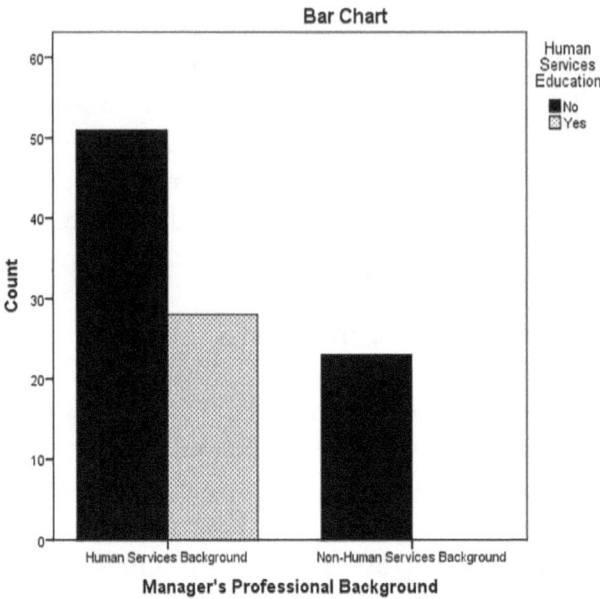

Figure 4. Cross-tabulation between human services degree held (yes or no) and the manager's professional background in human services (yes or no).

A χ^2 test was conducted to determine whether the association between holding a human services degree and having a professional human services background was statistically significant. The hypotheses were as follows:

H_0: The association between human services degrees and professional background in human services was not statistically significant.

H_1: The association between human services degrees and professional background in human services was statistically significant.

Results of the χ^2 indicated that the association between human services degrees and professional background in human services was statistically significant, $\chi^2 (1, 102) = 9.53, p = .002, \Phi = .33, p = .001$. The null hypothesis was rejected. Adjusted residuals, listed in Table 1, showed that there were significantly fewer degree holders without human services backgrounds than expected but also significantly more nondegree-holders without human services backgrounds than expected.

Table 1

Manager's Professional Background by Human Services Education Cross-tabulation

Manager's Professional Background		Human Services Education		Total
		No	Yes	
Human services Background	Observed count	51	28	79
	Expected count	57.3	21.7	79.0
	% within human services education	69%	100%	77%
	Adjusted residual	−3.4	3.4	
Nonhuman services Background	Count	23	0	23
	Expected count	16.7	6.3	23.0
	% within human services education	31%	0%	23%
	Adjusted residual	3.4	−3.4	
Total	Count	74	28	102
	Expected count	74.0	28.0	102.0
	% within human services education	100%	100%	100%

Descriptive Statistics for Summated Scales and Managerial Effectiveness

Recall that the Likert scale of agreement used to measure the three leadership behaviors of interest (i.e., objectives or goals emphasis, personal support, and work easing or facilitation) had a seven-point scale (1 = strongly disagree, 7 = strongly agree). Also, recall that summated scale scores were the means of each participant's responses to conceptually related items. Table 2 shows the descriptive statistics for the three summated scales and a measure of manager effectiveness.

Means for all three summated scales fell between 5 and 6 in value. Scores between 5 and 6 reflect responses between "somewhat agree" to "agree." The minimum score for all three summated scales was one, indicating that at least one participant strongly disagreed with all the survey items used to measure a particular summated scale. Alternatively, the maximum score for all three summated scales was 7, indicating that at least one participant strongly agreed with all of the survey items used to measure a particular summated scale.

The fourth measure, the descriptive statistics of which are listed in Table 2, summarizes overall managerial effectiveness. These data emerged from responses to the survey question, "How effective is your manager? Pleases choose one number between 1 and 10, with 1 = not at all effective, 10 = maximally effective." On average, participants rated managerial effectiveness between 7 and 8, indicating average perceptions were that managerial effectiveness fell between moderate and maximal.

Table 2

Descriptive Statistics for Summated Scales and Managerial Effectiveness

	Aims Emphasis SS	Personal Backing SS	Work Easing SS	Managerial Effectiveness
Cronbach's α	.74	.84	.94	–
Mean	5.59	5.31	5.46	7.64
95% CI LB	5.34	5.03	5.17	7.17
95% CI UB	5.83	5.59	5.75	8.11
5% trimmed M	5.69	5.42	5.60	7.85
Median	6.00	5.66	6.0	8.00
Variance	1.46	1.9	2.09	5.63
Std. deviation	1.21	1.40	1.44	2.37
Minimum	1.00	1.00	1.00	1
Maximum	7.00	7.00	7.00	10
Range	6.00	6.00	6.00	9
IQR	1.50	1.33	1.50	4
Skewness	-1.42	-1.28	-1.45	-1.05
Kurtosis	2.79	1.24	1.73	0.54

Note. 95% CI = 95% confidence interval of the mean. LB = lower bound of the 95% CI. UB = upper bound of the 95% CI. IQR = Interquartile range.

Correlations

This section shows the results of inspecting correlations to look for covariates and sufficient correlations among dependent variables to establish the analytical approach to answering RQs 1 to 3. The analytical plan was based on correlations: analyze RQs 1 to 3 with separate independent *t*-tests in the absence of covariates, analyze RQs 1 to 3 with one-by-two ANCOVA tests in the presence of covariates, analyze RQs 1 to 3 with a MANOVA test if the dependent variables (leadership behaviors: objectives or goals emphasis, personal support, and work easing or facilitation) were sufficiently correlated, or analyze RQs 1 to 3 with a MANCOVA test the dependent variables were sufficiently correlated, and there were covariates.

The patterns of the correlations among participants whose managers did and did not hold a human services degree are shown in Table 3. Correlations above the diagonal reflect managers without human services degrees, n = 73–75 participants. Correlations below the diagonal reflect managers with human services degrees, n = 27–28 participants.

The patterns across the two groups were identical. Four patterns emerged. One, all three summated scales (V1, V2, and V3) were strongly and positively correlated with each other. This justified a MANOVA test. Two, all three summated scales (V1, V2, and V3) were also strongly and positively correlated with the numeric estimate of the manager's overall effectiveness (V4). This justified a MANCOVA test. Three, there were strong and positive correlations between the years spent working for the current manager, years spent working for the current human services organization, and the participant's age (V5, V6, and V7). Four, these three demographic variables (V5, V6, and V7) did not correlate significantly with the summated scales (V1, V2, and V3) or managerial effectiveness (V4). Therefore, these demographic variables were not used as covariates.

Table 3

Pearson Correlation Matrix of Leadership Styles and Demographic Variables

	V1	V2	V3	V4	V5	V6	V7
V1 personal backing SS		.82**	.84**	.71**	.13	-.06	-.06
V2 aims emphasis SS	.71**		.86**	.75**	.14	-.02	-.07
V3 work easing SS	.84**	.92**		.81**	.19	-.05	-.02
V4 managerial effectiveness	.71**	.69**	.77**		.08	.02	.01
V5 years w current manager	.21	.19	.16	.15		.59**	.45**
V6 year w current organization	-.20	-.18	-.23	-.20	.66**		.48**
V7 age	-.03	-.09	-.04	.04	.35	.43*	

Note. V = variable. Above diagonal: managers without human services degrees, $n = 73–75$ participants. Below diagonal: managers with human services degrees, $n = 27–28$ participants. *Correlation is significant at the 0.05 level (2-tailed). **Correlation is significant at the 0.01 level (2-tailed).

Results for Research Questions 1–3

Correlations listed on Table 3 justified a MANCOVA test that addressed all three research questions at once in a single analysis. This section presents those results. RQ 1 was "Is there a difference in objectives or goals emphasis, as a leadership behavior, between nonprofit human services managers with and without human services degrees?" RQ 2 was "Is there a difference in personal support, as a leadership behavior, between nonprofit human services managers with and without human services degrees?" RQ 3 was "Is there a difference in work easing or facilitation, as a leadership behavior, between nonprofit human services managers with and without human services degrees?"

In the MANCOVA, the covariate was the managerial effectiveness. The independent variable was a human services degree, with two levels (yes, the manager held a human services degree; no, the manager did not hold a human services degree). The multivariate dependent variable was the linear combination of the three leadership behaviors of interest (aims emphasis, personal support, and work easing). MANCOVA first tests a set of multivariate hypotheses. The multivariate hypotheses were:

Covariate H_0: Managerial effectiveness was not a significant covariate.

Covariate H_1: Managerial effectiveness was a significant covariate.

Multivariate H_0: The difference in the linear combination of the three leadership behaviors of interest between managers with and without human services degrees was not statistically significant.

Multivariate H_1: The difference in the linear combination of the three leadership behaviors of interest between managers with and without human services degrees was statistically significant.

The data met the assumption of equality of covariance matrices, Box's M = 16.44, $F(6, 16,609)$ = 2.62, p = .021. The data also met the assumption of equality of error variances, aims emphasis SS Levene's $F(1, 99)$ = 0.52, p = .474; personal support SS Levene's $F(1, 99)$ = 0.12, p = .735; work easing SS Levene's $F(1, 99)$ = 0.95, p = .331.

Results of the multivariate portion of the MANCOVA showed that the managerial effectiveness was a significant covariate, Wilks λ = .35, $F(3, 96)$ = 60.29, $p < .001$; the covariate null hypothesis was rejected. The impact of the overall managerial effectiveness was very strong; partial η^2 = .65.

A STUDY OF MANAGEMENT LEADERSHIP QUALITIES WITHIN A NONPROFIT HUMAN SERVICE ORGANIZATION

When the impact of the overall managerial effectiveness was factored out, the difference in the linear combination of the three leadership behaviors of interest between managers with and without human services degrees was not statistically significant, Wilks $\lambda = .99$, $F(3, 96) = 0.37$, $p = .775$. The multivariate null hypothesis was retained.

Figure 5 illustrates mean ratings for aims emphasis across the two groups. The average rating for the aims emphasis SS was slightly higher among managers who held human services degrees, $M = 5.91$, $SD = 0.98$, than it was among managers who did not hold human services degrees, $M = 5.45$, $SD = 1.27$. Although the difference in means was nonsignificant, as per the MANCOVA results, the effect of human services degrees on this dimension of leadership was very strong, partial $\eta^2 = .45$.

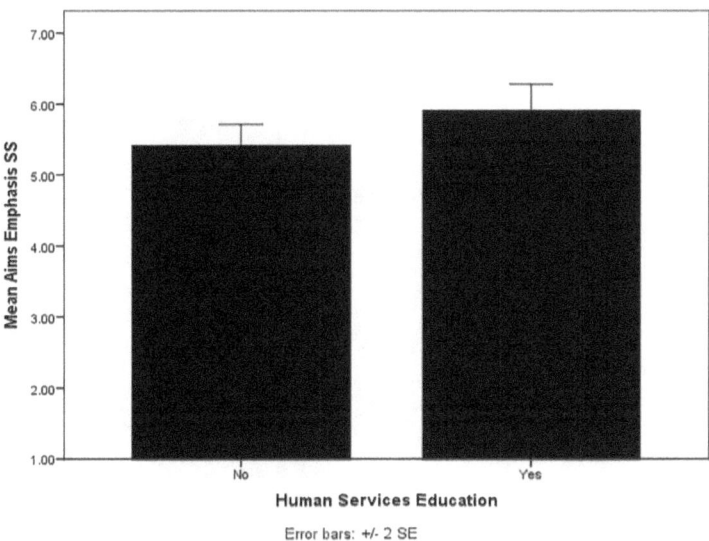

Figure 5. Mean aims emphasis SS across managers with and without a human services degree.
Note: Error bars: ± 2 SE

Figure 6 illustrates mean ratings for personal support across the two groups. The average rating for the personal support SS was slightly higher among managers who held human service degrees, $M = 5.71$, $SD = 1.40$, than it was among managers who did not hold human services degrees, $M = 5.15$, $SD = 1.45$. Although the difference in means was nonsignificant, as per the MANCOVA results, the effect of human services degrees on this dimension of leadership was very strong, partial $\eta^2 = .50$.

Figure 7 illustrates mean ratings for work easing across the two groups. The average rating for the work easing SS was slightly higher among managers who held human services degrees, $M = 5.79$, $SD = 1.28$ than it was among managers who did not hold human services degrees, $M = 5.30$, $SD = 1.49$. Although the difference in means was nonsignificant, as per the MANCOVA results, the effect of human services degrees on this dimension of leadership was very strong, partial $\eta^2 = .42$.

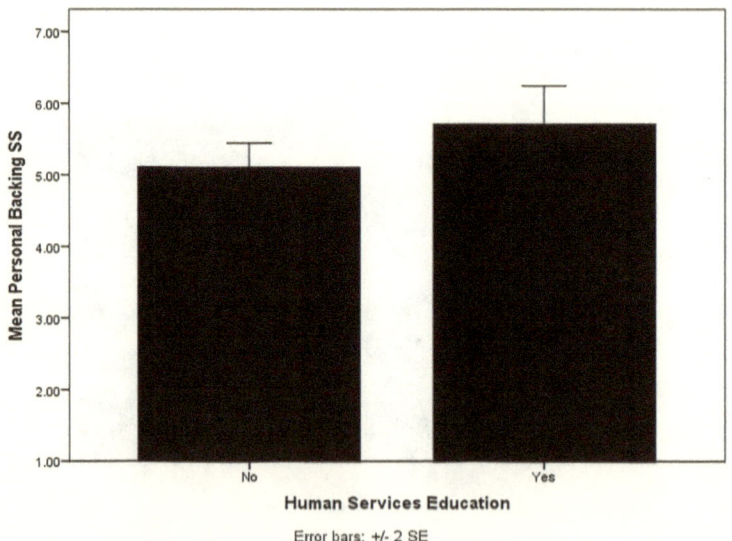

Figure 6. Mean personal support SS across managers with and without a human services degree.
Note: Error bars: ±2 SE

Answer to research questions

The answer to RQ 1 (is there a difference in objectives or goals emphasis, as a leadership behavior, between nonprofit human services managers with and without human services degrees?) was no. The answer to RQ 2 (is there a difference in personal support, as a leadership behavior, between nonprofit human services managers with and without human services degrees?) was no. The answer to RQ 3 (is there a difference in work easing or facilitation, as a leadership behavior, between nonprofit human services managers with and without human services degrees?) was no.

Ideal Nonprofit Leadership

Finally, participants were asked to identify the ideal nonprofit leadership by choosing from an array of four leadership styles on two survey questions, defined as follows:

Authoritarian: leaders who have an authoritarian management style have a high concern for the task and little concern for people.

Compromise management: Leaders who have a compromise management style have a moderate concern for the task and a moderate concern for people. This kind of manager attempts to stabilize the importance of completing the task while connecting to the subordinates and keeping them pleased since the team is usually effective, and they get along with the manager. Compromise managers are capable of eliciting respect from subordinates because they listen to and incorporate subordinates' ideas.

Transformational leadership: Leaders who have a transformational management style are involved with feelings, morals, values, and long-term goals.

Situational leadership: Leaders who have a situational leadership management style are rooted in the communication of relationship activities and task activities, in addition to employees' willingness or maturity in favor of performing a particular task.

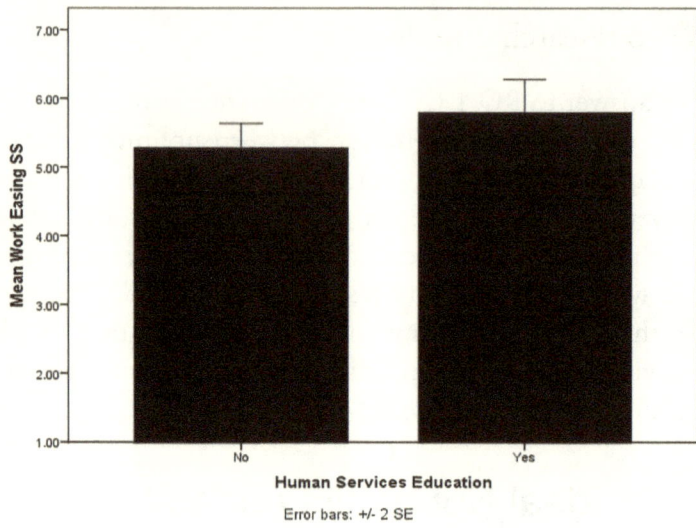

Figure 7. Mean work easing SS across managers with and without a human services degree.
Note: Error bars: ± 2 SE

Responses to the two survey questions were parsed out by group (human services managers with and without human services degrees) to determine if and how they differed.

Ideal leadership style for a nonprofit manager

One of the two survey questions was "What is the ideal leadership style for a nonprofit manager?" Figure 8 illustrates the percentages of participants in the two groups across ideal manager leadership styles. Table 4 lists the percentages and corresponding numbers of participants.

The majority of both types of participants (i.e., whose managers did or did not hold a human services degree) identified compromise management as the ideal leadership style for nonprofit managers (see Table 4). The type of style that garnered the next highest percentage of votes in both groups was transformational leadership. Finally, Figure 8 and Table 4 show situational leadership garnered the fewest votes. No one identified authoritarian leadership as the ideal style for nonprofit managers.

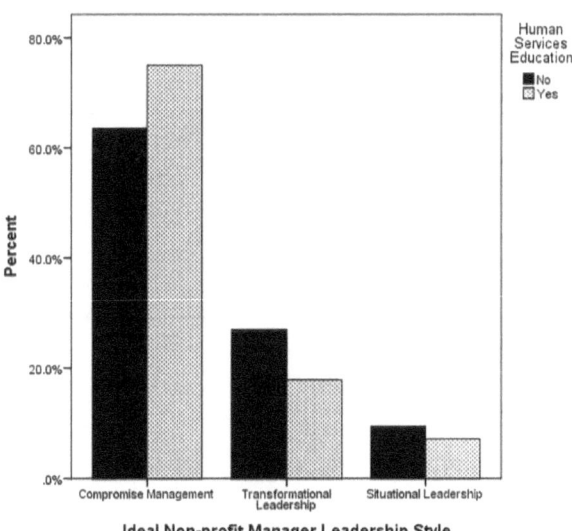

Figure 8. Percentages of participants in three ideal manager leadership styles.

Table 4 shows the percentages of participants who voted for the three leadership styles were close in value but not identical. Therefore, a χ^2 test of independence was conducted to determine if the percentages of votes for the ideal leadership style differed by testing the significance of the association between the cross-tabulated variables. The hypotheses were as follows:

H_0: The association between participant type (manager did or did not hold a human services degree) and preferences for the ideal nonprofit manager leadership style was not statistically significant.

H_1: The association between participant type (manager did or did not hold a human services degree) and preferences for the ideal nonprofit manager leadership style was statistically significant.

Table 4

Percentages and Corresponding Numbers of Participants by Ideal Nonprofit Manager Leadership Styles

	Ideal Nonprofit Manager Leadership Style		Ideal Leadership Type for Nonprofit Organization	
	Without Human Services Degree % (*n*)	With Human Services Degree % (*n*)	Without Human Services Degree % (*n*)	With Human Services Degree % (*n*)
Authoritarian	0% (0)	0% (0)	1% (1)	0% (0)
Compromise management	64% (47)	75% (21)	60% (45)	82% (23)
Transformational leadership	27% (20)	18% (5)	29% (22)	14% (4)
Situational leadership	9% (7)	7% (2)	9% (7)	4% (1)
Total	100% (74)	100% (28)	100 (75)	100% (28)

Results of the χ^2 showed the association between participant type (manager did or did not hold a human services degree) and preferences for the ideal nonprofit manager leadership style was not statistically significant, χ^2 (2, 102) = 1.22, p = .543, Cramer's V = .11. The null hypothesis was retained.

Best leadership style for a nonprofit organization

The other survey question was "Which leadership style is the best for a nonprofit organization?" Figure 9 illustrates the percentages of participants in the two groups across four ideal manager leadership styles. Table 4 lists the percentages and corresponding numbers of participants.

A STUDY OF MANAGEMENT LEADERSHIP QUALITIES WITHIN A NONPROFIT HUMAN SERVICE ORGANIZATION

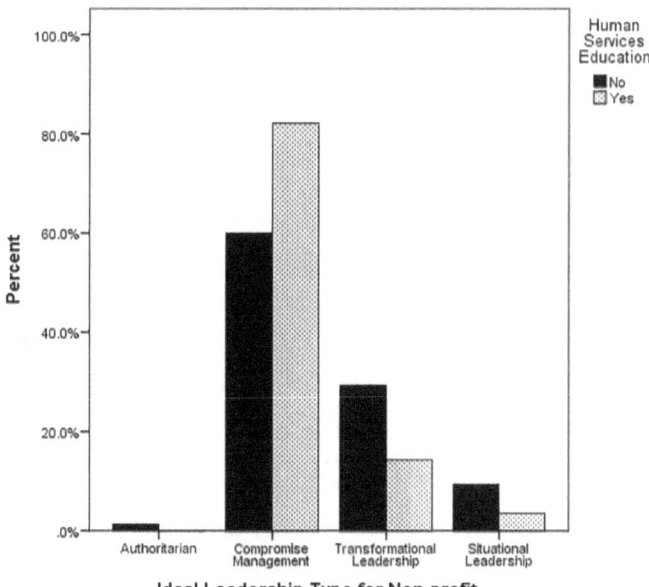

Figure 9. Percentages of participants in four ideal leadership types for nonprofit organizations.

Figure 9 shows one person in the group whose managers did not hold a human services degree chose authoritarian for the ideal leadership type of nonprofit organization. Otherwise, the majority of both types of participants (i.e., whose managers did or did not hold a human services degree) said compromise management was the ideal leadership type for nonprofit organizations (see Table 4). That was followed by transformational leadership. Finally, Figure 9 and Table 4 show situational leadership garnered fewer votes and authoritarian leadership only one vote.

Table 4 again shows the percentages of participants who voted for the four leadership types were somewhat close in value but not identical. A χ^2 test of independence was again conducted to determine if the percentages of votes differed. The hypotheses were as follows:

H_0: The association between participant type (manager did or did not hold a human services degree) and preferences for the ideal leadership type for nonprofit organizations was not statistically significant.

H_1: The association between participant type (manager did or did not hold a human services degree) and preferences for the ideal leadership type for nonprofit organizations was statistically significant.

Results of the χ^2 showed the association between participant type (manager did or did not hold a human services degree) and preferences for the ideal leadership type for nonprofit organizations was not statistically significant, χ^2 (3, 103) = 4.58, p = .205, Cramer's V = .21. The null hypothesis was retained.

Summary

The modal participant was a married Caucasian woman in her 40s who had worked for her current organization for 10 years and for her current manager for 5 years, N = 103 participants. Three times as many participants had managers who did not hold human services degrees, 73% versus 28%. A χ^2 test revealed a significant association between holding a human services degree and having a professional human services background, with fewer degree holders but more nondegree holders without human services backgrounds.

Means for three summated scales of aims emphasis, personal support, and work easing fell between 5 and 6 in value, reflecting "somewhat agree" to "agree" responses. Manager's effectiveness (measured on a 1–10 scale, where 10 = maximally effective) averaged 7–8, indicating managerial effectiveness fell between moderate and maximal.

Patterns in correlations among participants whose managers did and did not hold a human services degree were identical. Four patterns emerged: (a) all three summated scales were strongly and positively correlated with each other, (b) all three summated scales were strongly and positively correlated with the manager's overall effectiveness, (c) strong and positive correlations arose among demographic variables of years spent working for the current manager, years spent working for the current human services organization, and the participant's age, and (d) demographic variables did not correlate with summated scales or managerial effectiveness.

Correlational patterns justified a MANCOVA test that addressed all three research questions at once in a single analysis. RQ 1 was "Is there a difference in objectives or goals emphasis, as a leadership behavior, between nonprofit human services managers with and without human services degrees?" RQ 2 was "Is there a difference in personal support, as a leadership behavior, between nonprofit human services managers with and without human services degrees?" RQ 3 was "Is there a difference in work easing or facilitation, as a leadership behavior, between nonprofit human services managers with and without human services degrees?" MANCOVA results showed managerial effectiveness was a significant covariate. When its effect was factored out, the difference in multivariate leadership between managers with and without human services degrees was nonsignificant. For all three leadership summated scales, participants whose managers held human services degrees had higher means that reflected nonsignificant but strong effects of degree holders on leadership.

Finally, participants were asked to identify the ideal nonprofit manager leadership style and leadership type for nonprofit organizations. For both, the majority (60–82%) of participants identified compromise leadership as the ideal leadership style for nonprofit managers and organizations, followed by transformational leadership (14–29%), and situational leadership (4–9%).

The following chapter centers on the results, recommendations, and limitations of this study.

Chapter 5: Results, Recommendations, and Limitations

Purpose of the Study

The purpose of this research was to determine employee perspectives on the leadership behaviors of human services managers within a nonprofit human services organization. Specifically, this study intended to understand the effects of leadership style on employees in a human services organization located in the northeastern United States. This quantitative study was conducted by administering an online survey via SurveyMonkey to workers who gave direct care to patients in a nonprofit human services organization. A survey was disseminated to gauge if there was a correlation or dissimilarity in the leadership of managers who had didactic and professional backgrounds in human services versus those who had backgrounds unrelated to human services. Of 500 potential participants, a power analysis conducted on the GPower website calculated that 102 surveys were needed to find a common effect. However, 113 surveys were filled out. Of those, 10 participants failed to provide information on their managerial educational background, leadership style, or both. They were eliminated, so there were 103 surveys completed. The results of the data demonstrated there was one significant correlation flanked by education.

The reason for selecting 500 participants was to make/obtain quantitative analysis while at the sampling, the appropriate samples were selected, as the survey was conducted by using the online portal

A STUDY OF MANAGEMENT LEADERSHIP QUALITIES WITHIN A NONPROFIT HUMAN SERVICE ORGANIZATION

in which some of the employees provided accurate information and other employees may not have taken the survey seriously. Overall, the survey offers the complete details and the benefits of leadership in organizations.

A total of 113 individuals completed surveys. Of those, 10 participants (cases 4, 14, 20, 21, 33, 45, 62, 78, 101, 105) failed to provide information on their managerial educational background, leadership style, or both. They were eliminated from further analysis. The demographic results showed a modal participant was a married Caucasian woman in her 40s who had worked for her current organization for 10 years and her current manager for 5 years. There were 75 participants whose managers did not hold human service degrees and 28 participants whose managers held human service degrees. There was a 3-to-1 ratio of nondegree holders to degree holders. This is correct in general for human services organizations; because the majority of managers are taught what they are required to know to be successful in management is developed on the job. If not, they acquire, through their own experience, the knowledge and skills that are vital to their effectiveness. It showed there were significantly fewer degree holders without human services backgrounds than expected but also significantly more nondegree holders without human services backgrounds than expected. This was one of the observations that led the researcher to this study; one-quarter of the participants worked for managers who had neither formal education nor professional experience in human services. That combination of inexperience would make it difficult for someone to perform well at work.

Each participant was a member of one of the two groups: those whose managers held a human service degree and those whose managers did not hold a human services degree. They were asked if their manager's professional background included human services experience irrespective of formal education. Managers who had a human services background had a higher chance of being able to understand the needs of their employees due to the strong background.

DR. SHARON REED

Summary of Study

The success of an organization is based on the leadership behavior as the workflow of an organization is based on the performance of the employees. Leaders of an organization should have leadership skills so they will be able to manage the pre-consequences for the outcomes of the work. This research was based on the perspective of employees about the leadership, as the selected technique was quantitative because more employees could provide more useful information about the leadership at the specific organization. Previous researchers have described that leadership behavior is based on the performance of an employee; but somehow, if the behavior of a leader is suitable for the employees, the performance of the employees will be better. This is because when a leader appreciates an employee, the motivation level of employee increases so that he or she can do tasks with better effort (Raddats and Burton 2011).

This research provided the framework based on the results about how the leaders should behave with the employees in good or bad situations because difficulties are a part of any business; but if the leaders are influential, the outcomes will be positive. At some stages, the leaders should be able to make useful decisions for better performance; and in case an employee is not performing well, a leader should motivate that specific employee to boost the performance of the employee. The research information and the techniques have been described in the chapter entirely to ensure how this research can be more useful and effective for the leaders.

The first chapter served to give the framework that was essential to understanding the effects leadership qualities had on employees in human service organizations. This study intended to identify management factors that could improve the functioning of a nonprofit human services organization. The rising consciousness that leadership qualities are lacking in managers of nonprofit human services organizations developed into the concept of this study. The current research focused on leadership qualities in companies of profit, but there were also restricted studies on leadership qualities in nonprofit organizations.

A STUDY OF MANAGEMENT LEADERSHIP QUALITIES WITHIN A NONPROFIT HUMAN SERVICE ORGANIZATION

Reviewing countless studies seeking to identify the leadership qualities of individuals in supervisory positions within human service organizations, the canvasser determined where a gap in the current literature existed. This then developed into a research inquiry that appeared interesting and quantifiable: which of three activities (i.e., personal backing, objective emphasis, or work easing) do human service managers process, and in what essential qualities are they deficient?

Three research questions guided the hypothesis. They correspond to the three leadership behaviors of interest (aims emphasis, personal backing, and work easing). The hypothesis sought to ascertain how these variables related to one another and influenced leadership behaviors. Hypothesis one compared those with degrees, human services managers with human service degrees, or a background placing more emphasis on goals. Hypothesis two compared those with human service degrees, human service managers with no degrees, and only human services experience more focused on personal backing. Hypothesis three compared those with no human services degrees or preceding background process with the same emphasis on work easing. Therefore, the following hypothesis was based on the research question.

The second chapter presented a review of current leadership studies and practices. It also assessed the review of human services management and organizational ethos because it refers to the data analysis that can only be useful to organizations in the human services arena. Discussion of leadership was detailed since it is imperative to the success of any organization. An extensive analysis of leadership perceptions was presented since it formed the shape of how leadership skills affect employees. Leadership adds to the employees' sense of self-worth, employee burnout, gets the most out of personal promise, and then meets the goals of the organization better (Glisson 1989).

The third chapter explained the design of the study, including the utilization of a survey instrument, the company, and administration of the instrument, as well as the necessary sample size required to acquire accuracy. The approach for collecting data was discussed, including where the survey was conducted and how many rejoinders were needed to make sure the results were precise. The chapter also specified the questions utilized within the study and made clear how each hypothesis was addressed. The methodology for data analysis was also covered in chapter 3. It was determined that two-group analysis would be used, including *t*-tests, ANOVA., ANCOVA, MANOVA, or MANOVA tests to ascertain the relationships among the variables of leadership behaviors: aims emphasis; personal backing; and work easing.

The fourth chapter presented the analysis of the data that were acquired, utilizing the survey instrument. The data that were gathered included the use of a questionnaire and were presented on a question-by-question basis with the statistical verdicts of each overviewed and structured. Any correlations among variables were explored using correlations, chi-squares, and MANCOVA. The hypotheses were reviewed using the MANOVA to determine if conclusions might be drawn on the validity of each hypothesis. All hypotheses were inspected, the matching data were offered, and suitable suppositions made clear. Also, chi-square analysis was used to examine demographic variables about the managers' background in human services. The accurate results of the survey are conferred within segment 5.4.

Discussion, Results, and Conclusions

The effectiveness of research is critical because the selected topic directly interacts with the project's success. Employees are an essential part of an organization, as the whole workflow is dependent on the employees because if the performance is appropriate, the business or organization will be successful. Leadership factors are necessary to integrate into the organization because there are small teams in every organization, and a leader manages each team. Leadership interaction with the employees defines the consequence of the task or a project whereas the behavior of the leader in the workplace is also fundamental to organizational success. The research conducted provided results about the employees' perspectives on the behavior of leadership (Helgeson 2005).

In organizational leadership, there are two major things on which one focuses appropriately. First is about employers' focus on critical organizational consequences the employees use to arrange their interpersonal behavior regarding their organization. Second, the employee focuses on his or her perceptions, which are necessary for the employee's development. So that one can perceive several consequences about the organization, organizational leadership has a dimension that describes the influence of the social behavior where an employee can build a good social circle and interact with other people. So that can affect interpersonal skills, which can also lead them toward leader political skills, which are very useful for the management purposes of an organization. Another essential constraint an employee must control or must come up on is emotional exhaustion to implement the work in an organization appropriately.

Organizational regulations are usually violated by the behavior of an individual that may affect the organization, as well as its citizens. The organizational management can make some negative deviance whereas the effect is on the financial well-being of an organization, which may contain a significant loss to the organization. Positive deviance is the behavior the organization does not authorize unless that behavior helps the organization to achieve targets and goals. If positive deviance can help in this sequential purpose, an organization can give that behavior a title of the innovative behavior with dysfunctional derivatives. Negative deviance occurs in an organization because of absenteeism and workload on the employees. This negative behavior among employees can affect the desired target of an organization, either its profit or loss. An organization must face it very well; otherwise, it will be harmful for the organization (Birkinshaw and Morrison 1995).

When the ethical environment of any organization is good, the perceptions of employees depend on the management if the situation provided to employees is better than positive deviance and will be mentioned as an innovative behavior. Otherwise, negative behavior will affect the organizational behavior. In any organization, tactical leadership influences are also a major category that may create an ethical and pure political environment from which one gleans the connection of an article development. Influence tactics may distribute the workload of an employee or may increase the workload. That depends upon the number of tactics that are provided by the management system.

The demographic analysis showed a modal participant was a married Caucasian woman in her 40s who had worked for her current organization for 10 years and her current manager for 5 years. There were 75 participants whose managers did not hold human service degrees and 28 participants whose managers held human service degrees. There was a 3-to-1 ratio of nondegree holders to degree holders. This is correct in general for human services organizations because of the high turnover rate. The majority of what the human service organization's managers are taught, what they are required to know to be successful in management, is developed on the job. If not, they acquire, through experience, the knowledge and skills that are vital to their effectiveness. It showed there were significantly fewer degree holders without human services backgrounds than expected but also significantly more nondegree holders without human services backgrounds than expected. This is one of the observations that led the researcher to this study; one-quarter of the participants worked for managers who had neither formal education nor professional experience in human services. That combination of inexperience would make it difficult for someone to perform well at work.

Each participant was a member of one of the two groups: those whose managers held a human service degree and those whose managers did not hold a human services degree. They were asked if their manager's professional background included human services experience, irrespective of formal education. Managers who had a human services background had a higher chance of being able to understand the needs of their employees due to the strong background.

The study was to determine which of three leadership behaviors (i.e., personal backing, aims emphasis, and work easing) human service managers processed and what essential qualities were deficient.

A STUDY OF MANAGEMENT LEADERSHIP QUALITIES WITHIN A NONPROFIT HUMAN SERVICE ORGANIZATION

There were three associated hypotheses acquired from this question, and they are as follows.

Research question 1

Is there a difference in aims emphasis, as a leadership behavior, between nonprofit human services managers with or without human services degrees? Two survey items measured the leadership dimension of aims emphasis. An example of a survey question measuring aims emphasis was "My manager makes sure subordinates have clear goals to achieve." According to the sources and the research, it is clear that the aims and the goals emphasis, as a leadership behavior, is the crucial factor in an organization, and there are minor differences. But the leaders should bring both targets and the goals on the same platform so the results will be more effective.

Research question 2

Is there a difference in personal backing, as leadership behavior, between nonprofit human services managers with and without human services degrees? Three survey items measured the leadership dimension of personal backing. An example of a survey item that measured personal backing was "My manager is concerned about his or her subordinates." No personal backing exists in the leadership behavior because the leaders already have the skills to manage the consequences between the for-profit human services managers with and without human services degrees. It is about the ethical abilities of the leaders.

Research question 3

Is there a difference in work easing, as leadership behavior, between nonprofit human services managers with or without human services degrees? Four items measured the leadership dimension of work easing. An example of a survey item measuring work easing was "My manager helps his or her subordinates solve work-related problems." There was a large difference between easing and facilitation because the leader always preferred the facilitation, so the employees became motivated as they got proper incentives, so the outcomes were more effective and quality-oriented whereas work easing that focuses on the ability of the manager to help employees through solving work-related challenges can help an employee to feel more relaxed and committed to the organizational objectives.

All three research questions were addressed at once in a single analysis by using the MANCOVA test. Holding a human resources degree did not seem to increase the manager's effectiveness. However, valuable information was gained from the analysis. One of the critical aspects learned focused on the manager's overall efficiency matched their efficacy in three individual dimensions of leadership that were evaluated: aims emphasis, personal backing, and work easing. Other critical information that was obtained from the analysis was that the differences between managers with and managers without degrees were insignificant when the overall effectiveness of the managers was controlled. The analysis of the means showed there were differences among managers who had a degree across all the leadership behaviors that were investigated. Therefore future research should be designed to discover what managers without human services degrees and/or professional backgrounds engage their employees.

Limitations

As compared to previous research, this research is greatly optimized because the technique is quantitative, and the selected organization is having several experiences so the employees provided the information that will be useful while concluding the research. Leaders in an organization should need to be mentally stable to face the issues; also, the management of the employees should be considered a significant factor. In several types of research, the focus was based on the individual leadership in which the suggestions were appropriate; but as an organization, the employees' feedback is necessary because employees have complete interaction with the leadership, as well as the workplace. The leaders should initially analyze the current environment of the organization so they will be able to manage the workflow within the premises of an organization. This research provided a strategy for leaders who have departments to manage as the framework defines the issues that can be overcome and the constraints that should be followed by a leader in the organization (Mintzberg 1980).

The limitation of the research is based on the limited survey, as it has been mentioned above that the selected participants were surveyed from one nonprofit human services organizations; but if it was conducted as large-scale research, it could provide more useful results. But the conducted research was for small and medium enterprises as most of the leadership issues exist in the medium and small organizations. So the limitations can be overcome by conducting research on large enterprises for quality, assurance, and authentic information. Therefore, the results of this research are pertinent to a human service organization in this region. Nonetheless, this should be considered when applying the results to other human service organizations that do not fit this profile (Airman-Smith and Markham 2004).

The limitations of the research included the geographical area in which the study was conducted, the number of surveys taken delivery of, and only one organization was involved in the study. Therefore, the results of the analysis are pertinent to nonprofit human services organizations in this region. This should be considered when applying the results to other nonprofit human services that do not match the profile (Airman-Smith and Markham 2004).

One organization agreed to be involved in the study. Even though the organization was one of the largest in the state of Massachusetts, it allowed for a comparatively small number of managers to be rated based on the perceptions of their employees. So the limitations can be assuaged by conducting research on larger enterprises concerning the quality guarantee and authentic information.

Implications

This research implies human service agencies are able to enhance the effectiveness of their managers by understanding the connection between offering leadership behaviors (i.e., aims emphasis, personal backing, and work easing) to workers and possessing an academic background within human services. Organizations can make use of this information to narrow candidate choice, as well as look for supervisors who possess didactic backgrounds within human services. They can thoroughly assess their present managers to determine if workers who possess backgrounds within nonhuman-service fields could benefit from training in the human services arena so they may improve on understanding the direct-care providers within the human services arena and improve on following the direct-care providers, as well as persons who obtain these services.

Due to the drastic cuts in a budget that have been taken on nonprofit human services agencies, the government makes available most of the financial support for these programs. Therefore, the agencies have had to slash services to those in need of extra backing. If managers in these agencies were capable of gaining additional management and leadership skills, many costs could be reduced as they turn out to be more well-organized.

One way to ease some of the high staff renewal rates and burnout is through proper training. Within the human services arena, workers are exposed to a different way of life, as they see individuals prevailing over obstacles to turn out to be part of the community. By preparing individuals to work within this new ethos, it is less likely that an individual will leave as they will not undergo an attitude change of any type (Akdere and Schmidt 2007). Managers with subjective service backgrounds may well be exceptional trainers because their education is in providing backing to the people who require help and, therefore, may utilize this share of their education to educate their employees how to prepare to handle the different states of affairs that arise within this profession (Garski 2009).

Effects of leadership on the employees' behavior was also a concern of this research as the employees also followed the leader's behavior as most of the organizations were based on the institutes where the employees learned leadership skills from their leaders. Some employees were gaining an appropriate sense of leadership so they could get to know how to deal with the leaders. Leaders should not be very linnet because sometimes the strictness is necessary to achieve the current goals of the organization, as well as the market. Research has shown the leaders should play a neutral role, but sometimes difficult decision-making can help the leaders in their careers.

The worldwide administration aptitudes of conduct intricacy and stewardship improvement that add to corporate reputational capital are critical immaterial assets that lead to a practical advantage in the twenty-first century. Two exercises at the firm and industry-level on the effects of insufficient worldwide administration and squandered reputational capital were inspected. Four administrations' rehearsal to enhance key aggressiveness was given: universal authority abilities, official oversight duties regarding worldwide corporate notoriety, a yearly comprehensive reputational review, and extensive honors and rankings to concentrate energy on the elusive vital assets for a maintainable advantage in the twenty-first century.

An investigation of current administration hypotheses were displayed, alongside a synopsis of the significant writing discoveries. Accentuation is set on giving thoughts that have functional rather than hypothetical application. Another subject in the article is that authority aptitudes can be learned or educated, and the composition challenges organizations to actualize initiative improvement programs.

Recommendations for Future Research

Management in nonprofit organizations is based on many factors in which managers must be competent to maintain a higher level of performance. An important aspect that has been identified in this research is that leadership is an essential factor that defines a higher level of engagement within nonprofit organizations. The critical leadership behavioral traits that were investigated provided varying degrees of influence, especially based on the underlying factor that was being reviewed. Better decision-making within a nonprofit organization should be based on different understanding of essential concepts that have been included in this analysis. Therefore, crucial measures need to be investigated to provide a better understanding and help comprehend the findings from this analysis effectively. Developing a strong focus where it is possible to manage a nonprofit organization is based on the ability to identify fundamental concepts that have a significant role in their performance levels.

Future research should focus on determining the influence of different leadership styles within a nonprofit organization. This research has provided a very critical focus on how the overall leadership approach influences the level of employee engagement based on personal backing, work ease, and goal development. The significant focus on a specific leadership approach provides a different understanding of employee engagement considering that different leadership styles follow different organizational concepts, which focus on creating a highly engaged business environment. Thus, to provide accurate results, different types of leadership should be evaluated on the same dependent variable, which was the human services degree. The organization of research must reflect specific elements that are being implemented while ensuring the development of fundamental concepts that define successful knowledge of fundamental concepts that influence employee relations. Therefore, the success of employees within a nonprofit company is due to the leadership criteria adopted.

Future research should also focus on different nonprofit industries, such as health care, to determine the level of leadership efficacy based on the same variables. Health care would be the appropriate industry to provide useful comparative analysis considering it is easier to relate human services workers with health-care professionals despite operating in very different workplace settings. The research in health care would help in determining whether a change of leadership approach has different outcomes. The health-care environment is sensitive; thus, health-care leaders are also expected to be vulnerable in maintaining a strong focus on essential concepts that help define a better concentration on essential learning outcomes. Nonprofit organizations have different levels of engagement where it is easier to maintain strategic relationships between employees and employers.

Future research should be conducted in other nonprofit human organizations within the northeastern United States to build on this work to fully provide accurate results of leadership behaviors. Because only one human services organization was surveyed, this allowed for a comparatively small number of managers to be rated based on the perceptions of their employees. This will give better results for the managers' leadership skills in nonprofit organizations. Whereas individual managers can possess a natural set of strong leadership skills, for instance, task, relationship, and change behaviors, it will lend a hand to broaden the leadership skills that are lacking in human services and develop assessment skills that will enable the correct mix of behaviors for individual followers and states of affairs. Bear in mind that concerns for both persons and performance are significant.

Employee performance and leadership behavior are also important concepts that would be critical in successfully evaluating future research. Employee performance is essential and should form the basis under which better decisions can be made. This research would help in identifying critical leadership traits that have a positive influence on an employee, as well as the characteristics that have a negative effect on employee performance. The findings will be instrumental in informing leaders about the best approach when they want to maximize employee engagement. Different leadership behaviors have a distinct influence on employee performance. Definite integration of essential elements defines a successful operational setting where it is possible to achieve a higher level of success based on the expected. Therefore, the study development would be integral in determining the outcome.

Conclusion

The information about the complete framework of the leadership behavior has been described in the chapter as the research samples have been analyzed and described in the report for the appropriate quality of the research. Quantitative analysis has been discussed in the report for the better implication and the useful results of the leadership in the modern era. The knowledge has been described that leadership skills are the critical factor in organizational success. These findings can be utilized by present nonprofit human services organizations to build on their managers further. The results can also be used by canvassers to rely on further studies that continue to address the changing aspects of leadership in nonprofit human services organizations.

This research sought to investigate whether there was a difference in the quality of leadership investigated in nonprofit human services managers with and without degrees. The findings from the analysis showed there was only a statistically significant difference in one of the leadership behaviors that were investigated. There was a considerable difference in aims or goals emphasis between nonprofit human services managers with and without human services degrees. Therefore, leaders with human service degrees make sure subordinates have clearer goals to achieve than nonhuman services managers without human service degrees. However, there were no significant differences between human service managers with degrees and those without degrees in personal backing or work facilitation.

The recommendations made in this research are based on the findings and discussion of the outcomes. Human services managers should be well engaged in ensuring they maintain a robust interactive environment with their subordinates to help attain a higher level of organizational success.

Human services managers should focus on improving personal backing for their employees. Improving employee commitment within a given organizational context is essential in building strong positive relationships. Personal support involves showing concern about employees' personal issues considering that every employee has different needs. Maintaining positive relationships helps strengthen organizational performance.

Human services managers should focus on attaining human services degrees due to the specificity of the underlying concepts in managing employees. Even though the study has determined there was no significant difference across personal backing and work facilitation, goals formed the basis under which other critical organizational operations were developed. Therefore, ensuring they were instrumental in their mandate was based on a strategic understanding of fundamental concepts that defined successful development. Managers should be versitile to be effective in disseminating their mandate, as well as building better workplace relationships based on decisive measures that are implemented.

The selected topic of the research was considered the most critical topic because most of the small and medium enterprises are facing loss due to lack of leadership skills. The management of those organizations should conduct awareness sessions about leadership skills where the employees and the leaders learn to know how to manage a high-pressure situation in an organization because most of the issues exist due to lack of ability to handle pressure in an organization. The final recommendation is for research that can be conducted in the future to build upon the results of this study.

References

Abdel-Halim, A. A. "Interaction Effects of Power Equalization and Subordinate Personality on Job Satisfaction and Performance," *Human Relations* 32, no. 6 (1979): 489–499.

Airman-Smith, L., and S. K. Markham,. "What You Should Know About Using Surveys," *Research Technology Management* 47, no. 3 (2004): 12–15.

Akdere, M. and S. Schmidt. "Measuring the Effects of Employee's Orientation Training on Employee Perceptions of Organizational Culture: Implications for Organizational Development," *The Business Review, Cambridge* 8, no. 1 (2007): 234–239.

Arnold, K. A., N. Turner, J. Barling, E. K. Kelloway, and M. C. McKee. "Transformational Leadership and Psychological Well-Being: The Mediating Role of Meaningful Work," *Journal of Occupational Psychology* 12, (2007): 193–203.

Bass, B. M. *Transformational Leadership: Industrial, Military, and Educational Impact*. Mahwah, New Jersey: Lawrence Erlbaum 1998.

Bass, B. M. and Riggio. *Transformational Leadership* (2nd Ed.). Mahwah, New Jersey: Lawrence Erlbaum, 2006.

Bargal, D. and H. Schmid. "Recent Themes in Theory and Research on Leadership and Their Implications for Management of the Human Services," *Administration in Social Work* 13, no. 4 (1989): 37–54.

Beauchamp, T. L. "A Defense of the Common Morality," *Kennedy Institute of Ethics Journal* 13, no. 3 (2003): 259–317.

Birkinshaw, J. M. and A. J. Morrison. "Configurations of Strategy and Structure in Subsidiaries of Multinational Corporations," *Journals of International Business Studies* (1995): 729–753

Blanchard, K. "Situational View of Leadership," *Executive Excellence*, no. 8 (1991): 22–23.

Bolman, L. G. and T. E. Deal. *Reframing Organizations: Artistry, Choice, and Leadership* (3rd Ed.). San Francisco, California: Jossey-Bass/Wiley, 2003.

Boneva, B., R. Kraut, and D. Froehlich. "Using E-mail for Personal Relationships," *American Behavioral Scientist* 45, no. 3 (2001): 530–549.

Bowers, D. G. and S. E. Seashore. "Predicting Organizational Effectiveness With a Four-Factor Theory of Leadership," *Administrative Science Quarterly*, no. 11 (1966): 238–263.

Brotheridge, C. M. and S. Long. "The 'Real-World' Challenges of Managers: Implications for Management Education," *The Journal of Management Development* 26, no. 9 (2007): 832–844.

Campbell, D. T. and J. C. Stanley. *Experimental and Quasi-experimental Designs for Research*. Chicago, Illinois: R. McNally, 1963.

Capowski, G. Anatomy of a Leader: Where Are the Leaders of Tomorrow?" *Management Review* 83, no. 3 (1994): 10.

Carney, B. M. "Breaches of Confidentiality and the Electronic Community Health Record: Challenges for Health Care Organizations and the Community," *HEC Forum* 13, no. 2 (2001): 138–148.

Cohen, J. *Statistical Power Analysis for the Behavioral Sciences* (2nd Ed). Hillsdale, New Jersey: Erlbaum, 1988.

Conger, J. A. "Charismatic and Transformational Leadership IN Organizations: An Insider's Perspective on These Developing Streams of Research," *Leadership Quarterly* 10, no. 2 (1999): 76–84.

Cosmides, L. and J. Tooby. "Knowing Thyself: The Evolutionary Psychology of Moral Reasoning and Moral Sentiments," *Ruffin Series in Business Ethics* (2004): 93–128.

Creswell, J. W. *Research Design: Qualitative, Quantitative, and Mixed Methods Approaches* (2nd Ed.). Thousand Oaks, California: Sage, 2003.

This book encourages critical thinking and motivates the reader to process beyond the normal way of thinking and educates on the power of conditioning and how trained thoughts have impacted the people of America. It is a resourceful tool that gives brief historic occurrences that impact America and the rest of the world to this very day. This book provides enlightening details of how America operates that ultimately impacts all who live within America and all over the world.

No information is effective without solutions to follow. The writer gives solutions to every flaw we have endured from the impact of American conditioning and encourages a higher level of thinking. The writer challenges you to look beyond what we have been taught and to find the rewarding treasures of knowledge that have always been accessible for all mankind.

As in all American history, the book carries you into the hard and dark truths that impacted black people of America and how we must never erase or forget the history, but rather learn and elevate from it. Dare to embrace painful truths as you have cherished embracing a lifetime of myths and lies.

By erasing ignorance and spreading knowledge, we will finally begin to heal as an entire nation from the negative impact of America. When we know better, we do better.

$19.95

Daft, R. L. *Management* (7th Ed.). Mason, Ohio: South-Western, (2003).

DelCampo, R. G. "The Influence of Culture Strength on Person-Organization Fit and Turnover," *International Journal of Management* 23, no. 3 (2006): 465–469.

Department of Human Services, Dane County. (2008). Retrieved on January 15. http://www.danecountyhumanservices.org.

Dittrich, J. E. and M. R. Carrell. "Organizational Equity Perceptions, Employee Job Satisfaction, and Departmental Absence and Turnover Rates," *Organizational Behavior and Human Performance* 24, no. 1 (1979): 29–42.

Dias, J. J. and S. Maynard-Moody. For-Profit Welfare: Contract, Conflicts, and the Performance Paradox," *Journal of Public Administration Research and Theory* 17, no. 2 (2007): 189–211.

Dubrin, A. J. *Leadership: Research Findings, Practice, and Skills* (4th Ed.). New York, New York: Houghton Mifflin, 2004.

Eisenberger, R., G. Karagonlar, F. Stinglhamer, P. Neves, T. E. Becker, M. G. Gonzalez-Morales, and M. Steiger-Mueller. "Leader-Member Exchange and Effective Organizational Commitment: The Contribution of Supervisor's Organizational Embodiment," *Journal of Applied Psychology* 95 (2010): 1085–1103.

Fowler, F. J. Jr. *Survey Research Methods: Applied Social Research Methods Series* (3rd Ed.). Thousand Oaks, California: Sage, 2002.

Garski, J. S. *A Study of Three Leadership Behaviors of Supervisors in Two Nonprofit Human Service Organizations.* Capella University, 2009.

Gliner, J. A. and G. A. Morgan. *Research Methods in Applied Settings: An Integrated Approach to Design and Analysis.* Mahwah, New Jersey: Erlbaum, 2000.

Glisson, G. A. "Dependence of Technological Routinization on Structural Variables in Human Service Organizations," *Administrative Science Quarterly* 23, no. 3 (1978): 383–394.

Glisson, C. "The Effect of Leadership on Workers in Human Service Organizations," *Administration in Social Work* 13, no. 3/4 (1989): 99, 116.

Graen, G. and J. F. Cashman. "A Role-Making Model of Leadership in Formal Organizations: A Developmental Approach. in James G. Hunt and Lars L. Larson (Eds.)," *Leadership frontiers,* 143–165. Kent, Ohio: Kent State University Press, 1975.

Greene, L., and G. Burke. "Beyond Self-Actualization," *Journal of Health and Human Service Administration* 30, no. 2 (2007): 116–127.

Hair J. F. Jr., W. C. Black, B. J. Babin, R. E. Anderson, and T. L. Tatham. *Multivariate Data Analysis.* Upper Saddle River, New Jersey: Prentice Hall, 2010.

Harel, G. H. and L. K. Conen. "Expectancy Theory Applied to the Process of Professional Obsolescence," *Public Personnel Management Journal* 37, no. 2 (1982): 143–158.

Havighurst, C. C., P. B. Hutt, B. J. McNeil, and W. Miller. "Evidence: Its Meanings in Health Care and in Law," *Journal of Health Politics, Policy, and Law* 26, no. 2 (2001): 195–219.

Helgeson, S. *The Web of Inclusion: Architecture for Building Great Organizations.* Washington, DC: Beard Books, 2005.

Hersey, P. and Blanchard, K. "Great Ideas Revisited: Revisiting The Life-Cycle Theory of Leadership," *Training and Development* 50, no. 1 (1996): 7–42.

Holloway, B. J. "Leadership Behavior and Organizational Climate: An Empirical Study in a Nonprofit Organization," *Emerging Leadership Journals* 5, no. 1 (2012): 9–35.

Hughes, R. L., R. C. Ginnet, and G. J. Curphy. *Leadership: Enhancing the Lessons of Experience.* New York, New York: McGraw-Hill, 2006.

Humbley, A. M. and B. D. Zumbo. A Dialect on Validity: Where We Have Been and Where We Are Going," *The Journal of General Psychology* 123 (1996): 207–215.

Institute for Social Research. Ann Arbor, Michigan: The University of Michigan, 1975.

Jones, K. "Transformational Leadership for Transformational Safety: Developing a Transformational Style Begins with These Four Dimensions: Influencing, Inspiring, Engaging, and Challenging" *Occupational Health and Safety* (2006).

Katz, R. L. "Skills of an Effective Administrator," *Harvard Business Review*. Boston, Massachusetts: Harvard Business School Publishing Departments, 1974.

Koontz, H. C. O. and H. Weihrich. *Essentials of Management* (4th Ed.). New York, New York: McGraw-Hill, 1986.

Kotter, J. P. *A Force FOR Change: How Leadership Differs from Management.* New York, New York: Free Press, 1990.

Lindberg, J. S. "DRO Contingencies: An Analysis of Variable-Momentary Schedules," *Journal of Applied Behavior Analysis* 33, no. 2 (1999): 123–138.

Maak, T. "Responsible Leadership, Stakeholder Engagement, and the Emergence of Social Capital," *Journal of Business Ethics* 74, no. 4 (2007): 329–344.

Meers, K. A. "Contextual Barriers TO Strategic Implementations: An Examination of Frontline Perceptions," *Journal of American Academy of Business* 11, no. 2 (2007): 11–17.

Mintzberg, H. "Structure in 5s: A Synthesis of the Research on Organizational Design," *Management Science* 26, no. 3 (1980): 322–341.

Mohamed, S., and H. N. Nguyen. "Leadership Behaviors, Organizational Culture, and Knowledge Management Practices," *Journal of Management Development* 30, no. 2 (2011): 206–221. Retrieved from ProQuest. doi: ISS 0262-1711.

Morris, M. H., D. F. Kuratho, and J. G. Covin. *Corporate Entrepreneurship and Innovation* (2nd Ed.). Mason, Ohio: Thomson South-Western, 2008.

Newman, M. A., M. E. Guy, and S. H. Mastracci. "Beyond Cognition: Affective Leadership and Emotional Labor," *Public Administration Review* 69, no. 1 (2009): 6–20.

Northouse, P. G. *Leadership Theory and Practice* (2nd Ed.). Thousand Oaks, California: Sage, 2001.

Raddats, C., and J. Burton. "Strategy and Structure Configurations for Services Within Product-Centric Businesses," *Journal of Service Management* 22, no. 4 (2011): 522–539.

Shapiro, J. P. and R. E. Hassinger. "Using Case Studies of Ethical Dilemmas for the Development of Moral Literacy;

Towards Educating for Social Justice," *Journal of Educational Administration* 45, no. 4 (2007): 451–470.

Siegel, S. and N. J. Castellan Jr. *Nonparametric statistics for the behavioral sciences* (2nd Ed.). New York New York: McGraw-Hill, 1988.

Sluss, D. M., R. E. Ployhart, M. G. Cobbs, and B. E. Ashforth. "Generalizing Newcomers' Relational and Organizational Identifications: Processes and Prototypicality," *Academy of Management Journal* 55 (2012): 947–975.

Toor, S. and G. Ofori. "Leadership Versus Management: How They are Different and Why," *Leadership and Management in Engineering* 8, no. 2 (2008): 61–71.

Trevino, L. K. and K. A. Nelson. *Managing Business Ethics: Straight Talk About How to Do It Right*. Hoboken, New Jersey: John Wiley & Sons, 2011.

Truitt, T. *Exploring Effects of Innovation Management: A Selective Study of Nonprofit Managers' Perceptions*. Northcentral University, 129, 2007.

University of Michigan, Survey Research Center. *Michigan Organizational Assessment Package: Progress Report II*. Ann Arbor, Michigan: Survey Research Center, Institute for Social Research, University of Michigan, 1975.

Warner, R. M. *Applied Statistics* (2nd Ed.). Los Angeles, California: Sage, 2013.

Weber, M. C. "Home and Community-Based Services, Olmsted, and Positive Rights: A Preliminary Discuss," *Wake Forest Law Review* 39, no. 1 (2007): 269–277.

Weinberg, M. "A Case for an Expanded Framework of Ethics in Practice," *Ethics and Behavior* 15, no. 4 (2005): 327–338.

Weisbrod, B. A. "The Future of Nonprofit Sector: Its Entwining with Private Enterprise and Government," *Journal of Policy Analysis and Management* 16, no. 4 (1997): 541–555.

Wren, J. T. *The Leader's Companion: Insights on Leadership Through the Ages*. New York, New York: Simon & Shuster, 1995.

Yukl, G. A. *Leadership in Organizations* (2nd Ed.). Englewood Cliffs, New Jersey: Prentice Hall, 1989.

———*Leadership in Organizations* (6th Ed.). Upper Saddle, New Jersey: Pearson Prentice Hall, 2006.

About the Author

Dr. Sharon Reed was born and raised in Pittsburgh, Pennsylvania; she was a special education teacher before shifting to leadership, is a first-time author, and graduated from Argosy University in Phoenix, Arizona, with a doctorate in education. She now lives in Brockton, Massachusetts, where she spent many years as an educator and managing many programs. When it comes to people, being a strong believer of leadership and empowering people to take ownership of their positions and processes is the key to leadership.

www.ingramcontent.com/pod-product-compliance
Lightning Source LLC
Chambersburg PA
CBHW030844180526
45163CB00004B/1441